What people are saying about …

DREAMING OF MORE FOR THE NEXT GENERATION

"Dr. Michelle Anthony has become a tour de force on her mission to equip this generation's families and church leaders with the resources required for genuine transformation through intentional discipleship. In *Dreaming of More for the Next Generation*, Dr. Anthony gently but deftly dismantles the juggernaut of today's well-intentioned but fatally flawed family ministry models by exposing their biblical insufficiency and deflating results. She then provides protein-rich principles and examples of church-equipped but parent-empowered family ministry designed to nurture authentic faith. Through her imminently accessible and intimately personal style, Michelle helps church leaders and parents reimagine faith formation in ways that resonate with clarity and authenticity. It has become clear to me, as an astute observer of her writing, that she is building an interlocking body of work through each successive book that is being assembled into a new and comprehensive paradigm for family ministry. Having been an eyewitness of her ministry impact in the local church and within her own family, I can attest to the fact that these principles are practiced by her and embodied in the lives of many. Let me invite you to drink deeply from the new wine that has refreshed me and many others."

Freddy Cardoza, PhD, chair of the Christian Education Department at Biola University and Talbot School of Theology, and executive administrator of the North American Professors of Christian Education

"*Dreaming of More for the Next Generation* is an important book with deep and rich theology for children's and family ministry leaders. Not only were the wheels in my head turning with ideas, but my heart was stirred with longing for a genuine movement of families being formed by the Holy Spirit, shaped by a powerfully unified community of faith, and awakened to the story God is telling and the part they are to play. *Dreaming of More for the Next Generation* challenges leaders to reexamine their tightly held ministry models and submit them to God for something more: more organic, more Spirit-led, more focused, more bold, more formative, and more intentional. I pray for you as you read this book that you will hear from God and He will transform your life, your family, and your ministry beyond your wildest dreams."

Matthew Guevara, campus pastor at Christ Community Church, Chicago, Illinois

"God is seeking bold leaders who are willing to change the way we shape the next generation for Jesus. As a church leader, father, and grandfather, I know that our top priority must be to put God in the center of our homes. *Dreaming of More for the Next Generation* gives practical insights to church leaders and hope for parents as we endeavor to spiritually shape our kids. I am confident this book will help all who read it make a difference in generations to come … and into eternity."

Gary Webb, executive pastor of ministries at Northwoods Community Church, Peoria, Illinois

"Michelle Anthony has truly pioneered a new and successful approach to family ministry with *Dreaming of More for the Next*

Generation. Throughout the last several years, Michelle has inspired, equipped, and supported today's churches on how to awaken parents to their biblical roles while at the same time awakening the church to the supportive role it plays in nurturing faith in this next generation. This book is a must have for today's churches wrestling with defining 'family ministry' and struggling with practicalities of infusing new, innovative, and God-inspired philosophy into locked-in traditional methods and practices."

Tommy Larson, families pastor at ROCKHARBOR church, Costa Mesa, California

"Out of her own real-life journey as a parent and ministry leader, Michelle awakens us to new dreams of catalyzing lifetime faith in the next generation. She engagingly invites us to explore new 'wineskins' in partnering with parents and the Holy Spirit. Our church family has deeply resonated with her visionary blueprint of *what can be* in the transformational adventure of family ministry."

Scott Benson, executive pastor of ministries at Friends Church, Yorba Linda, California

"I love how practical and intentional Michelle is in equipping church leaders to help parents become successful spiritual leaders. Even after working in children's ministry for over twenty years, I still felt unsure and overwhelmed in leading my own children. These practical steps have helped me to be a better parent and the spiritual leader the Lord calls me to be, both in my home and in my ministry."

Cheryl Howard, associate pastor to children and families at Mariners Church, Irvine, California

DREAMING OF MORE

FOR THE NEXT GENERATION

Lifetime Faith
Ignited by Family Ministry

michelle anthony

David C Cook®

transforming lives together

DREAMING OF MORE FOR THE NEXT GENERATION
Published by David C Cook
4050 Lee Vance View
Colorado Springs, CO 80918 U.S.A.

David C Cook Distribution Canada
55 Woodslee Avenue, Paris, Ontario, Canada N3L 3E5

David C Cook U.K., Kingsway Communications
Eastbourne, East Sussex BN23 6NT, England

All personal stories throughout are used with permission.

Unless otherwise noted, all Scripture quotations are taken from the Holy
Bible, New International Version®, NIV®. Copyright © 1973, 1984, 2011
by Biblica, Inc™. Used by permission of Zondervan. All rights reserved
worldwide. www.zondervan.com. Scripture quotations marked ESV are taken
from The Holy Bible, English Standard Version® (ESV®), copyright © 2001
by Crossway, a publishing ministry of Good News Publishers. Used by
permission. All rights reserved. Scripture quotations marked WE are taken from
THE JESUS BOOK—The Bible in Worldwide English. Copyright SOON
Educational Publications, Derby DE65 6BN, UK. Used by permission.
The author has added italics to Scripture quotations for emphasis.

LCCN 2012935341
ISBN 978-1-4347-0016-2
eISBN 978-1-4347-0536-5

© 2012 Michelle Anthony

The Team: Don Pape, Karen Lee-Thorp, Amy Konyndyk,
Nick Lee, Caitlyn York, Karen Athen
Cover Design: Jonas Barber

Printed in the United States of America
First Edition 2012

1 2 3 4 5 6 7 8 9 10

032912

To my husband, Michael
Your inspiration and support of
me gave my dream wings!
I'm forever grateful!

ACKNOWLEDGMENTS

To write a book that spans a ministry journey of over twenty-five years entails a great amount of gratitude to so many people. I think back to my formative years at First Baptist Church of San Jose, where I caught a vision for how children's and youth ministry could make a lasting impact on young people, and am thankful for people who invested in me, such as Brad Chinn, Barbara Weber, and Jim Cook. It was Lyle Castellaw who gave me my first opportunity to lead in youth ministry, and Michael Anthony who believed I could teach and who trained and mentored me to do so.

Colleagues such as Cheryl Howard, Cristi Thomas, Charles Molenkamp, KJ Stephens, and Sean Anderson gave wings to the dream that children's and youth ministries could work together for the sake of the family. In God's sovereignty, it was ROCKHARBOR Church, with leaders Todd Proctor, Stacy Scott, and the elder board, who said yes to a dream … when it was only that. I will be forever indebted to Kit Rae for the partnership that gave me hope for the long road ahead, to the tireless support of Tommy Larson through endless seasons of change, and to Matt Barnes for being willing to stay in the trenches with me at every step.

Thank you to David C Cook, who invested in the dream of family ministry for the sake of spiritual formation—especially to Marlene LeFever for bringing me there in the first place; to my most incredible boss, Dan Rich (you never cease to amaze me with your servant and strong leadership); partners such as Byron, Mike, Jana, Janet, Jenn, and Ruth, who have added their fingerprints along the way. And to my audaciously creative and hardworking Tru team: Debbie, Cristi, Tori, Leigh, Matt, Patti, Jonas, Joel, Brad, Cory, Jen, and Stephanie, whom I'm so honored to be leading and serving alongside. Each of you inspire me every day! Thank you, Stacy and Angelina, for hanging in there and never giving up, for giving honest feedback, and for sacrificing so much.

Thank you to Don Pape and Terry Behimer for believing in this project and to Karen Lee-Thorp for your insight and encouragement.

I'm grateful to my parents for always praying for me and the ministries I have been called to; my husband, Michael, for being my champion at every turn; and my children, who made me want faith for this generation more than anything else.

I am truly grateful to be a part of such a long legacy of individuals who have also had a dream … a dream for more!

CONTENTS

1

A NEW WINESKIN

The Dream of Family Ministry

You are never too old to set another
goal or to dream a new dream.

Les Brown, Live Your Dreams

It was a milestone, for sure. I had just completed twelve years in children's ministry. My staff, volunteers, and family showered me with cards and words of affirmation. My boss had even given me a crystal clock. I had arrived. An *entire generation* of children had been born and had grown up—and now those children were in middle school. I had watched it happen. I had led it, for all practical purposes.

Twelve Vacation Bible Schools and twelve summer camps; six hundred and twenty-four weekends with lessons to study, crafts to prep, and volunteers to recruit; twelve fall recruitments; twenty-four parent meetings; thirty-six all-church announcements; five 9-1-1 calls; hundreds of first-time decisions; countless pagings of parents for crying babies; and dozens of revisions of budgets and ministry plans. You know the drill. It's a lot—but I love it.

So I sat there at my desk, looking at my crystal clock, and a series of haunting thoughts crept over me. An entire generation of kids—were they *different* after this ministry we had created for them? Would their faith last *beyond* their childhood? Would they *change* the world with the love of Christ? Did our programs, sleepless nights, tireless efforts, countless dollars, and careful screening of staff and volunteers pay off?

I Want More

I must confess that deep inside, I wasn't sure of those things. I was sure the kids had had fun. They had been given excellence. They knew songs and Bible stories. They had memorized verses. They had made friends. They had loved our programs, themed rooms, and cool T-shirts.

I feel embarrassed sharing this, but I believe there is someone else out there who may have felt this way too. I simply got caught up in doing a lot of really good things. And by the grace of God, He chose to use those good things. But in the end, I didn't want to sacrifice another twelve years to just have "good." I drove home that night with tears in my eyes, asking God, "So what do I do now? I want *more*!"

Faith in the Home

There are moments in our lives, both professionally and personally, when we know we are sitting at a crossroads. That night, for me, was one of them. Would I continue in ministry to children, or would I try something else? If I did the former, I knew that there was something *more*. At the time, I just didn't know what it was. I begged God to show it to me and to my team. Our hearts were right. We wanted to serve Him and invest in this generation, but we weren't seeing the results that we were hoping to see. We were discouraged. We needed divine intervention.

Both of my children were young, and I was intentionally investing in their faith in a multitude of ways in our home: family nights, mission trips, serving opportunities, time in God's Word, prayer, and times for them to gain an authentic glimpse into my own faith journey. One night we had one of my daughter's friends over for dinner, and she participated in our family night. When her mom came to pick her up, our night together opened up a spiritual conversation. This mom was curious and interested. Over the next few months, I had the privilege of leading her to faith in Christ. What followed shaped the answer to my question about my ministry to children.

Spiritual Parents

This woman and her family were now on a spiritual journey—together. The mom barely knew what it meant to have a relationship with God, let alone how to lead her daughter spiritually. It took intentional discipleship for her to understand how God was spiritually parenting her, and how to spiritually parent in the same manner.

This was it! This was what was missing in my children's ministry! An intentional plan to equip parents both in their spiritual lives and in their roles as spiritual parents. God was awakening me and our ministry to His heart for the family—and our family ministry, in its feeble beginnings, was birthed.

The Doorsteps of Home

The pursuit of forming spiritually minded children who own a vibrant faith drove us to the doorsteps of the home. As leaders, we had to assess the ways in which we had portrayed Christ's call to faith. Most of us know the sobering statistics of the current generation's faith formation and their commitment to it beyond their teenage years. As the church sits in dismay of how this could possibly happen on our watch, parents, too, are shocked that they did "the best they could" and still remain disappointed with their children's faith.

Every day, countless young people leave the church and, worse, abandon their faith for something "more" in North America. What has been our response? More programs? Better curriculum? Stricter accountability to godly behavior? I wanted to understand how we had been led to believe that faith is simply knowing the right information about Christ and acting with good behavior.

Perhaps no one would *actually* say that. Of course we would say that we wanted a faith that impacted all we did and said, faith that would last a lifetime. But think about it: if faith is simply about good teaching and proper behavior, then the church *is* a sufficient place for children to learn that. But if faith is that *plus more*—if it is understanding how to *live out* what we believe in real time, by the power of God's Spirit over a lifetime, then the family (with spiritually minded parents), would be the best place for that!

In chapter 6 we will look deeper into the kind of faith that we are talking about here, but for now, we want to highlight the idea that faith is established when someone has a *firm conviction* (not just good information) and has chosen to *personally surrender* all rights and privileges of his or her life in submission to God (not just "good behavior"). Both the conviction and the surrender in one's life involve a supernatural transformation that God does within us (from the inside out) as we choose to obey Him one step at a time. And often along the way, we misstep as well, which is why grace is such an important part of faith. In our children's ministry, we needed a shift not only in our thinking, but in our ministry applications as well so that this kind of faith formation, accompanied by grace, was being cultivated.

New Wineskins

In many ways, the paradigm shift from "achieving proper behavior" to "a life posture of faith formation from the inside out" in the ministries for our children could be compared to Jesus's words about embracing a new wineskin:

> Neither do men pour new wine into old wineskins.
> If they do, the skins will burst; the wine will run
> out and the wineskins will be ruined. No, they
> pour new wine into new wineskins, and both are
> preserved. (Matt. 9:17)

His original audience would have understood an old wineskin as one that had already expanded during the fermentation process of new wine. This expansion would have taken place when the bladder being used was still fresh and pliable. Once expanded, it had dried out. To put new wine into an old wineskin would cause it to crack or burst open. Those listening to Jesus would have known that you put new wine in new wineskins for it to be beneficial.

Jesus used this image to compare the religious system prevalent in His society with the "new wine" He was about to pour out. The new wine was an opportunity for people to no longer have to "earn" a relationship with God through observance of the Law but rather to "experience" God in a relationship through the power of His Spirit, who was poured out after Christ's death satisfied the price of sin.

This paradigm shift in thinking and acting required a new understanding. The old ways of doing things would no longer be useful for what was to come. In fact, those not interested in the new wineskin would lose out on both the new covenant and the relationship with God.

Bag of Tricks

It might be tempting for us to look at this and say, "Who would be foolish enough to do *that?*" Well, in fact, I am. Perhaps you are too. Perhaps you went into ministry with unbridled passion, or maybe you signed up reluctantly and quickly found that nothing else would satisfy what you were created to do. Whether you were mentored or you stumbled upon your niche through trial and error, eventually we all arrive at "what works." I call it our "ministry bag of tricks." The longer you have been in ministry, the bigger your bag! In our hearts, we want to see lives changed. We are passionate about it. We want to make sure we're using the things in our bag that *work*.

Then one day God's Spirit begins to do a new thing; He wants to pour out a new wine. But we find ourselves skeptical. Why should we change? It's always worked well in the past, right? The moment we are seduced by the things of old, the new wine is not ours to taste. We get nostalgic. We remember the ways that God used the things in our "bag"—they were the things we prayed for, and He answered. We get very comfortable with our old wineskin. After all, it has seen a lot of miles with us. We are old friends.

The Cost of Laying It Down

There are practical matters, too. How will my church respond to this new wineskin? What if my supervisor or pastor doesn't agree with it? What if I lose my job? Along with fear, insecurity can creep in too. For me, it had been eight years since my awakening to ministry where I was investing in kids and their parents and was intent on faith formation as the goal. Now God was asking me once again to lay down my old wineskin *completely*. I had moved to a new position at a different church. As I arrived, convinced that God wanted to pour out His new wine upon this ministry, equipping parents and the family as primary, I still warred against my raging insecurities.

As I took over the leadership of our children, youth, and families, I was tempted to show up on the first day with my big bag of tricks. Oh, was it ever big! There was hardly room in my office for me or anyone else when this trunk of treasures arrived. History? I've got history—in fact, here's a binder with VBS notes from over a decade ago, just in case. Experience? I've got experience—here are my degrees, books, and events that I planned in the past. Ideas? Plenty of those—let me just find them here in this bag, somewhere. And don't forget how many people have loved my ideas in the past. *Just saying.*

For some reason, my new staff didn't care about my bag. What was worse was that in my heart, I knew that none of it was going to work if God was going to start pouring out that new wine. Thirsty for what was to come, I put the bag aside. At first it was close, "just in case." But over time, it was all but eliminated from view. The old wineskin was finally gone, and now we were ready for what God had in store for us.

Together we watched as the new wineskin took shape, and we waited in anticipation and humility for God to fill us with what we needed. And He did! After over twenty years of ministry to children and their families, everything I was doing was new! What an adventure! We would ask God, and He would respond—and children, leaders, and parents were being *transformed*.

We knew we needed a new standard of measurement, not necessarily at the end of the lesson, weekend, or even quarter, but rather growth markers over the lifetime of a child's faith. How might we perceive faith formation if our view was further out than next weekend? In part, what was needed for such an evaluation required the very thing we wanted to instill in our children in the first place: *faith*! We needed the robust kind of faith with deep roots if we were going to be successful at this. We would not be able to settle for its counterfeit.

Faith's Counterfeit

Many years ago, when my children were little, my husband and I made our way through the local swap meet and its myriad of stalls. On this Saturday morning in December we had one goal in mind: to find stocking stuffers. The objective was simple—lots of stuff, little money. We were impressed with our bags of what "looked like" designer sunglasses, radios, watches. Our son and daughter were *kids*—they wouldn't know the difference. Besides, the items would soon break, and this way we wouldn't have spent a bundle.

What we didn't anticipate was how quickly those things would break once we gave them to our children. Within the day, most of what we had purchased had cracked, not worked, shrunk, or failed to offer what it promised in some way. The old adage that you get what you pay for was true, but what struck me more was how closely these items had resembled the real thing. And in the end they were counterfeits and couldn't stand up to the pressure that our children imposed on them.

The same conclusion could be made about good behavior. It often resembles the "real thing"—faith—but it cannot stand up to the pressures that life will certainly impose upon it. Only true faith withstands trial.

So what might God be doing in this generation to germinate faith in the lives of children and their families? How is He calling us to embrace authentic faith rather than its counterfeit, good behavior? I say its counterfeit, because one must look very closely to see the difference sometimes. They manifest themselves in such similar ways. Think about it. We applaud good behavior. We reward it without question of motive or heart. After all, it is God who judges the heart, right? And faith, when mature, produces good behavior, so essentially it's the same thing, right? Wrong. This is the very point that Jesus was getting to in His example of the new wine and wineskins. Religious behavior is not what He looks for—not then, not now. He is looking for faith!

The Greenhouse

As I took that long, hard look at my ministry to children and their families with these two lenses—a genuine partnership with parents, and authentic faith formation—I knew we had work to do. Well, God had work to do in us, to be more specific. We recognized that faith comes from truth and a vibrant, submissive life in relationship with God Himself. But faith is also designed to grow best (especially in the early years) in the home. Think of a greenhouse. Certainly a plant can grow out in the harsh elements of life and nature, but it grows *best* in a greenhouse, where all the elements are optimum.

God's intent for the family is for each generation to pass on faith to the next. So not only did He say that faith was the primary thing that He would expect from us someday, but He also set up an infrastructure that He envisioned would be best for this type of replication: the family.

Partly out of ignorance, much of my past ministry had eliminated parents from experiencing their God-given role of nurturing faith. There were even times when, out of compassion, I felt that we as the church could *help parents out* by doing what they were struggling with. New-wineskin thinking helped me evaluate my ministry by a different standard. Instead of "rescuing" children from the lack of spiritual parenting they were receiving, I began to think in terms of "raising up" spiritual parents and homes.

Parents Awakened

How does a church come alongside parents to help them in their own faith formation so that the spillover of their faith influences their children in the way God envisions? And what shifts in ministry focus need to take place in order for us to devote time and attention to a ministry for adults when our infrastructure was designed for children and youth? Such questions are at the core of embracing a new wineskin, and they will be the foundational questions of this book.

Parents and ministry leaders can so quickly succumb to manipulating kids into good behavior and forgetting what really fosters faith: a relationship with God. We must arrange our ministries at the church and at home to teach and model that faith comes from *experiencing* God. It's not formulaic, not packaged and sitting on a shelf somewhere. It's organic and fresh.

Think of Saul, an epic student of God and His Word, a Pharisee among Pharisees. His transformation occurred when he *experienced* God. We have been entrusted with this generation of young people and have the privilege of placing them in the path of the Divine, where His divinity transforms. His holiness changes everything. Even today, we can create environments where we put God on display in all things.

Family Ministry Models for Faith Formation

In chapter 3 we'll look in more detail at what's involved in making parents primary in faith formation, and in chapter 4 we'll unpack the terms *faith formation* and *spiritual formation* to see what they do and do not mean. But even now, begin thinking about a ministry approach that best fits your church. Here are four models of how family ministry can be expressed in a local church.

Family Friendly

In this model, the church's programmatic structures for children and youth are unchanged, but each separate ministry creates opportunities to draw generations together and encourages parents to participate in their children's discipleship through events and trainings.

Family Sensitive

"Family ministry" is a department in this model, focusing on responding to the urgent needs and issues that today's families are dealing with. It makes the healing of the family primary. Ministries are organized in separate departments with little intergenerational interaction.

Family Empowered

Although age-organized programs and events still exist in this model, the church is completely restructured to draw generations together. The goal is to equip parents and champion their position as primary disciple makers. The church takes a supportive role in this endeavor.

Family Centered

In this final model, the church has eliminated life-stage programs or events. The worship service and other events are multigenerational with a strong emphasis placed on the parents' responsibility to spiritually nurture their own children. The entire community feels a part of the faith development of the next generation whether they have children or not.

Awakened to More

We often hold on to those ratty old wineskins because we think they represent our dreams. But God is offering us *more*! And once we taste the new wine, we always want more. Recently I moved to another position and left that office where I once showed up with my security blanket of my bag of tricks. As I was packing up, I found that material. And realized that I hadn't used it in six years. I smiled as I threw it all, piece by piece, into the trash. I am now anxiously waiting for God to give me a new wineskin once again.

MINISTRY ASSESSMENT

Take time to reflect, respond, and dream about how God might want to awaken you to *more* in your life personally or in your ministry to children and their families.

Reflect

How would you describe your current wineskin? When did your journey with it begin? How has it shaped you? Borne fruit? How did you see God bless it? In what ways can you see that it might have hindered faith formation in children's or families' lives? Why? What might be disconcerting about laying the old wineskin down to embrace a new one? What might the new one look like? Describe what your ministry could look like if God chose to pour out His new wine upon it? Spend some time writing an account of your thoughts and reflections.

Respond

Take some time to respond to God based on the things that He has revealed to you. Is this a time of confession or celebration? How will your response reveal where your faith is today? Is this a time for quietness and solitude? Or is this a time for you to have a conversation with a member of your team or a family in your ministry for support or encouragement? However God's Spirit is speaking to you right now, respond to Him in that with a heart of surrender.

Dream

What dreams might God be dreaming for you? Are there dreams you desire that can be put into words? Is there a particular next step that you can begin implementing immediately? A person you could share this dream with? How might the things God has revealed to you serve as a catalyst to make some adjustments in your ministry to children and their families? As you look at the four models of family ministry, which model is God leading you toward in your ministry today? Is there a blend of the models or a new model? Where can your journey be shared or translated into a ministry opportunity?

2

SEVEN PILLARS OF FAMILY MINISTRY

··

A Foundation to Build Upon

Every Christian family ought to be as it were a little
church consecrated to Christ, and wholly influenced
and governed by his rules. And family education and
order are some of the chief of the means of graces. If
these fail, all other means are likely to prove inef-
fectual. If these are duly maintained, all the means
of grace will be likely to prosper and be successful.
Jonathan Edwards, The Works of Jonathan Edwards

Perhaps you are still dreaming about what it would look like to begin
building a family ministry. Or maybe you have already embraced the

concept and are drawing up the plans. No matter where you are in architectural design, it's always a good idea to assess the foundation.

Our homes and churches are only as solid as the foundation we build them upon. And when the home and the church narrow the dividing line between them, faith is able to penetrate into all aspects of life, destroying the separation between the sacred and the secular. This is the beauty of family ministry. This chapter will explore seven core ideas that have become foundational for family ministries within the local church, regardless of what model we choose. I call them the Seven Pillars, and each of the remaining chapters of this book will align with one of these pillars.

Pillar One: Family Is Primary

When we start discussing parents as the primary nurturers of their children's faith, many ministry leaders say to me, "I'm not sure our parents are ready for that yet." My response is that they became ready for that the moment they had children. This is not my idea. This is God's idea. God is the One who said faith formation would primarily take place in the home.

I recognize that we have broken families with an abundance of troubling issues. But that doesn't let parents off the hook. It doesn't discharge them from their God-given role to be the primary people who pass on the faith to the next generation. So we need to fully embrace the role laid out for us in Ephesians 4:11–13. We need a plan to come alongside and *equip* parents to do *their* ministry in tangible ways. We need to pray for God to awaken parents to this role. We need to do this even in the midst of dysfunction, because dysfunction will always be with us.

In chapter 3 we will look at practical examples of how to awaken and equip the parents in your ministry.

Pillar Two: Spiritual Formation Is Our Goal

We desire that those in our care will have been spiritually formed by the time they leave our ministry. In chapter 4 we'll explore in detail what that means, but fundamentally it refers to what Paul said in Galatians 4:19:

> My dear children, for whom I am again in the pains
> of childbirth until *Christ is formed in you.*

We want *Christ formed in you* in every child in every children's ministry, in every student in every student ministry, and in every home. We want *Christ formed in you,* nothing less.

I believe that spiritual formation is more than just information and that the pursuit of life transformation for our children over a long spectrum of time is the best measurement of faith. So if you're a children's pastor, middle school pastor, high school pastor, or family pastor, there's never been a day when we've needed to work *together* more.

We have to start looking at the family holistically and borrowing from one another knowledge and information about each family unit. We need to look at each child and student within the context of his or her family, not just as an individual. And when a child or student comes into our ministries and they're not attached to a family, then it's our job to spiritually form them and become family to them. It's a lifelong transformation process. In chapter 4 we'll unpack a basic definition of spiritual formation that will give you a framework for creating a transformational ministry, and we'll look at things that can thwart transformation from reaching maturity.

Pillar Three: The Holy Spirit Is the Teacher

In the children/family ministries I have led, we have chosen not to call our leaders "teachers." We call them storytellers of God's Big Story. We reserve the holy role of Teacher for the Spirit of God. Sometimes by just changing language, we can change the way we approach a situation. Our language reminds children that the Spirit is their Teacher even when they're not in our classes or our homes.

It's essential to teach them to rely on Him at all times. Our job is simply to create environments where He can work, to come alongside what God's Spirit is already doing. I like to use the metaphor of a sailboat: our job is just to hoist up the sail as wide as we can, so that as God's wind is blowing in a child's life, we get to come alongside that. We catch the wind. And even though the sail is important, sometimes we focus too much on our sail—our ministry or approaches or curriculum or training. That's important, but it's not nearly as important as the wind. Not a lot of sailing is going to happen on water where the wind isn't blowing, so we desperately need Him to blow. Our job is just to cooperate with that.

Chapter 5 will give you greater understanding of how the Holy Spirit can work in your ministry and in the individual lives of your children, and how they can learn to hear from God and respond accordingly.

Pillar Four: Scripture Is Our Authority

The authority of Scripture is crucial. We need to make sure we're teaching truth in a culture that denies it. Without truth, people are lost. They have no compass. Arguably this generation is more in need of the authority of Scripture in their lives than most that have preceded them. These young people need to become students of the Word. So our task is not just to teach kids about God's Word, but also to allow them to investigate it for themselves.

It's critical to give them opportunities to put the Word into practice, to let them test it until they feel confident that they can defend it against a hostile world. By creating environments where children are not only hearers of God's Word but doers also, we allow them to flex their faith muscles in ways that bring validity to the truths we have taught them. When they experience faith in action for themselves, its power is ingrained in them forever. Chapter 6 offers practical examples of how to allow children opportunities to put their faith into action.

Pillar Five: The Big God Story

One of our central ministry tasks is to unpack the big narrative, God's Word, as one redemptive storyline with one main character. When we share it chronologically throughout the year as an unfolding narrative, kids begin to see that there is indeed one mastermind behind it all, and He alone is God. There is great power in teaching the narrative chronologically, conveying a sense of the whole with a beginning and a trajectory in time, rather than merely studying Daniel this week and Moses next week.

In chapter 7 we will discover the awe-inspiring strength of a generation that understands the entire gospel from beginning to end, that is awake to a story that's *still being written* and the part they can play in it.

Pillar Six: God Is Central

God should be the main focus of everything we do. What we want to teach kids is not just the pieces of the story, but also how to know God personally through those pieces. What keeps our children's faith vibrant for the long haul is an actual relationship with God.

God is at the center of the story. What do we know about God and His character from any given part of the Big God Story? These things will ultimately form us. The things that biblical people did, or that people in our lives do today, all serve as examples of how God's character is actively at work.

In addition, throughout history God has called His people to pause in annual festivals for the sake of remembering and celebrating Him and acknowledging Him in the midst of daily living. Today we still have this need to pause to remember and celebrate. What can this look like in our culture and families today?

And what about celebration and worship? With God at the center of teaching, then our worship is a response to Him. Creating space for children to experience God by responding to Him in worship is essential for relational faith development.

Chapters 8 and 9 will explore creating traditions for the sake of remembering and celebrating and will delve into cultivating a heart of worship as response to God. You'll find practical examples for implementing each value in your ministry setting.

Pillar Seven: Ministry Support

Many of us are leading our ministries through change. Changing programs, values, staffing, and focus. And we have probably spent far too many years in ministry slugging it out by ourselves, on the verge of either burnout or discouragement. Creating teams of volunteers and leading a unified staff toward a common goal through seasons of change are among the challenges and blessings in this ministry endeavor of passing on our faith to the next generation.

Psalm 78 commissions us to pass on faith from generation to generation, even to those *yet to be born*. Faith that lasts will take more than just me or you or our local church. We're going to have to join together for the long haul and *not give up*.

Chapters 10 and 11 will help you lead in a season of change while providing volunteer and staff development toward your goals.

MINISTRY ASSESSMENT

How will you design a ministry based on the principles in these pillars, but specifically crafted for your church and your people, and with God's dreams for you? As you prepare to dive into the following chapters, take some time to think through each of the pillars and the ministry dream that God has placed on your heart thus far.

Reflect

Which of these pillars are strong in your ministry? Which are not so strong? What is God saying to you about them? In what ways has God awakened you to a potential blind spot in your current ministry? What are areas that you have tried to implement but have become discouraged or disenchanted about? What have been your barriers to success? Where have you seen God's Spirit lead you forward in confidence? In victory?

Respond

How do you sense God moving you today? What is one next step that you can take? What words describe your heart toward God's movement of spiritual formation in this generation right now? What image best describes your family ministry as it is today? What part might God be asking you to play in that process?

Dream

If you could see ten years into the future, what would be your hopes for the adult children in your ministry today? How would their places of education and work describe them? What is your dream for the condition of the family in the twenty-first century? What do you desire for God to say about your role in ministry at the end of your season of serving?

AN AWAKENING TO PARENTS AS PRIMARY

....

Cultivating Spiritual Parents

The church must assume the role as a training
ground for parents to be the soul doctors for
their children … in order to bring spiritual
healing. Parents must learn how to really be pres-
ent with their children and to create space for
contemplation and reflection in their homes.

Holly Allen, Nurturing Children's Spirituality

Perhaps you are like me: everywhere I turn, someone is having an inspiring discussion about family ministry and the need to raise up spiritual parents in the home. You may be thinking, *This is great, I*

get it—but what about the parents? *They are the ones who don't get it.*
How can the church begin to make progress in family ministry if our
parents aren't as passionate about this as we are?

Or why does it seem that 99 percent of parents will attend a
back-to-school night at their child's school, while only 3 percent
will attend a parent vision meeting at their church? We need parents
who are awakened! Parents who hunger for more than merely getting
through the day. We have the privilege of helping them be awakened
to their role by inspiring them with this envisioned future. It's time
for us to pastor, shepherd, be winsome, and be inspiring!

Sense of Relevance

Recently I was online looking at the wide array of help books for
parents. There is something for everyone: books on ADD, bedtime,
discipline, defiance, curfew, complaining, bed-wetting, biting,
finances, friends, fighting in the car (an entire book about managing automobile arguments!), manners, media, potty training—you
name it. There are even books promising that you can literally fix
everything wrong with your child in one week.

These are the issues that control the very lives of our parents—
these issues are *relevant* to them. Each day is spent accomplishing a
vast list of important and not-so-important tasks. As the church, we
need to help awaken our parents to their God-given role, helping
them to see that the spiritual vitality of their life and their child's life
is relevant. Until they do, they won't assume this role.

The church is poised to inspire and shepherd parents to not
merely spend their hours but invest their days during these critical years of child rearing. There is so much riding on this need for

parents to step up and lead their children in spiritual matters. In fact, George Barna said, "Every dimension of a person's experience hinges on his or her moral and spiritual condition."[1] Think about it—what you believe and where you aim your heart determines the direction and outcome of your entire life *through eternity*. Eternity is at stake. What is more relevant than that?

Parents often think that if they hide in the shadows long enough, we will let them off the hook. At first we think they are being lazy or stubborn or even apathetic, but I've come to realize that most parents do *want* to assume their spiritual role—they just don't know *how*. They feel scared and insecure, and they, more than anyone, know their imperfections. This is why we must graciously remind them that spiritual parenting is not *perfect* parenting … but rather imperfect parenting from a *spiritual perspective*. This means parenting with eternity in mind.

Empowered Families

The church needs family-empowered ministries not only to raise up a generation of faith followers but to *raise up a generation of spiritually minded parents* as well. Parents today need the church to inspire them, equip them, and support them in this incredible endeavor. I now judge my ministry by how well I am equipping parents toward this role.

We need a community where we all hold each other accountable to these things:

- Parents are the *primary nurturers* of their children's faith; the faith community plays a *supportive role* in this endeavor; and the Holy Spirit is the One who works *when and as He chooses* in the life of a child.

- We will equip and disciple parents with the *same intentionality* that we have equipped and trained our volunteers in the past.

- We will strive to become a *family of families* where every member plays a role in the spiritual nurturing of the children in the community.

Let's unpack each of these premises as well as explore practical examples of how they might look in a church setting.

Parents as Primary

Most parents and ministry leaders don't argue the point that God's Word calls parents to be the primary spiritual leaders to their children (Deut. 6; Ps. 78). Nor do most have issue with the mandate of the church to be an equipping entity (Eph. 4:11–12). Rather, the problematic issue is *how* this actually works in our current culture and society.

I reached one such point of tension in my ministry when I found that I had placed the words *We believe that parents are called by God to be the primary nurturers of their children's faith* in our statement of faith. I remember looking at this one day on our church's website and thinking, *How can I honestly say that I believe that when I have done little or nothing to display this belief?* Furthermore, I considered the ways that I had unknowingly sabotaged that value by having the church play the primary role and the family play a supportive role to us.

Here are a few of the glaring examples that God graciously brought to my attention that day.

Take Home versus Pre-Teach

We provided take-home papers after a child's time in Sunday school. While nothing is inherently wrong with a follow-up resource, I began to see that this sent the wrong message to my parents. Without saying it directly, I was communicating that we would be the primary teachers of God's Word and they would support us by reinforcing the message at home.

I became passionate about inverting the process. We would create a pre-teach resource where parents would be the first ones to read the upcoming week's Bible passage to their children and interact with them on it. Then, when their child came to church, we would support what they were teaching in the home and be the ones to follow up with a service on that topic. Now, instead of parents asking, "What did you learn in *church* today?" we, the ministry leaders, were able to ask the children, "What did you learn at *home* this week?"

What about those children whose parents can't or don't engage in the pre-teach? For them it's no different than the way we have always done it. If we change nothing, all of our children will come to church thinking that we are the ones who are the primary teachers, but if we make this pre-teach adjustment, we will at least capture some of our families to think of their role as primary. We have nothing to lose and so much to gain.

Faith Classes

Like many churches, our children's ministry offered classes for elementary kids on new faith, baptism, and serving. Working from the church-is-primary perspective, I faithfully taught these classes. Parents would drop off their children on Sunday afternoons with a sack lunch and come back two hours later. Of course the parents were grateful, faithfully did the homework with their kids, and brought them back the following week. At the end of the course, we would host a graduation ceremony, and parents would join us to celebrate their child's achievement.

However, if parents were to be primary, then I would need to revise this model. We began to offer these classes for children, but they would attend with a least one parent (or grandparent, in some cases). When they arrived, my role would not be to "teach" the class but rather to "facilitate" it. We made copies of the handouts with the "answers" in them for the parents, and the children had the blank copies. This way, we could set our parents up for a win by allowing them to have the information that they would need ahead of time.

As facilitators, we did a little instruction, gave examples, and posed different questions, but the parents were the ones who were looking up Scripture with their children and praying alongside them in discovery. There was even a time set aside when parents found a quiet place in the church where they could share with their child how they came to know Christ. As parents and children returned to the room, there was not a dry eye among them. I can't imagine the conversations that were now open because we chose to support the parents in being seen as spiritual leaders to their child.

Child Dedications

While this next one may vary in your church, depending on your denomination, the concept is replicable. In our church we offer child dedications for parents who wish to formally dedicate their children to the Lord at a young age. In the old wineskin model, the parents brought their child on stage, where our pastor and elders prayed blessings over them. Again, there is nothing wrong with this, and in fact it is how I dedicated my own two children. But as we considered parents as primary in our context, we wondered if there was *more*.

We tried many different options to allow our parents to assume a greater role. We had them choose a life verse and blessing for their child that they spoke over the child publicly while the pastors confirmed it with a supportive prayer. We also tried a separate service on a Saturday morning where families came for two hours with relatives and friends for an extended and focused time of dedication. In the latter example, parents were not herded through a ten-minute space in front of many in the church body whom they didn't know. Rather, space and time were given to each member of the family to offer blessings—sometimes three generations of blessings. Our pastoral staff joined them to offer Scripture and prayers as well as a time of fellowship. Our parents have been affected in tremendous ways as they prepare for and remember this special day of anointing.

A Blessing

At the conclusion of our children's services, we offer a blessing to each child as a benediction. The word *benediction* literally means "good speaking" and is most often translated "blessing." Numbers 6:24–26 records the Lord instructing Moses to bless the people with these words: "The LORD bless you and keep you; the LORD make his face to shine upon you and be gracious to you; the LORD lift up his countenance upon you and give you peace" (ESV).

A simple but very powerful way to empower parents as spiritual leaders is to inspire and equip them to give a daily blessing to their child. This can be a prayer they pray over their child, although the language is slightly different. In a traditional prayer we commonly address God directly, for example, "Dear God" or "Dear Jesus." A blessing often states things that are prayerful in nature but declare truth about God or the life He has called us to, such as, "May you know that God's protection and love is always with you," or "Go in His peace."

We model this for our parents at all-church family events and give them the opportunity to put it into practice as a community so that they feel confident in it. We also encourage them to place their hand on their child's shoulder, head, or arm and look them directly in the eye when they speak. It's always a wonderful time to affirm their love by saying, for example, "Micah, your father loves you very much." Whether at bedtime, or in the morning before everyone leaves for the day, offering a blessing can be a lifelong gift.

The Most Important Part

Stating that parents were primary allowed us to intentionally think through how we could play a supportive part. But the final and most important piece is that it's the Holy Spirit who transforms lives when and as He chooses. We must never deviate from this by thinking that if we invert our paradigm we will arrive at transformation almost formulaically. No! It will always be as we align ourselves with the Spirit's work.

Paul told the Philippians that this process happens in cooperation with the Spirit, since He is the One who gives us the power and the desire to obey (Phil. 2:13). Our role, therefore, is to equip parents to cooperate and participate with the Spirit's work, to come alongside that which God is already doing in the lives of His children. What a liberating way of looking at the roles of pastoring and parenting!

Same Intentionality

The next area of investigation for us had to do with how much time I had spent in developing volunteers. Our ministries are full of volunteer recruitment, screening, training, appreciation, follow-up, caregiving, and even discipline and removal at times. We read books about volunteers, and there are hundreds to choose from.

Volunteers are enormously valuable. They are the backbone of the church. We couldn't pull off a weekend service without them, so we seek to develop them at every turn. But in our ministry, we discovered that we hadn't demonstrated that same *intentionality* toward parents.

Where could we bring parents into strategic places in our ministry, taking into account their busy lives? Where were we training and developing them for their spiritual roles in the home, and where were we offering them our affirmation, encouragement, and caregiving?

Spiritual Parenting Class

One of the first things I started was a class for parents called *Spiritual Parenting*. (The content of that course is now available in book and DVD form as a resource for churches to do the same.) This course allowed me to share scriptural values about their role. In those weeks together, we were inspired, convicted, equipped, and supported to take the next step. Over time, this course gave an identity and common language to our parent community, unifying us on the same mission.

My friend Patti started a Spiritual Parenting class at her church and was surprised at what God did: "I offered this class because that's what a good Family Pastor does. And my parents attended because that's what good parents do too! But then each one of us left *changed*. We were blindsided by God's Spirit showing up, training our hearts in what it meant to nurture children spiritually, and we all left with a sense of awe and peace, knowing we weren't in this alone."[2] Since then, Patti has had the opportunity to have refresher gatherings once a month to keep the conversation going. This has allowed her to stay in her role of equipping and supporting the parents in her community.

Family Nights

One of the most challenging decisions I ever made during this time of transition was to not offer a midweek program. Again, there is nothing wrong with a midweek program, and many fulfill the exact values that we are discussing here. But in our church community, this extra night out was a distraction from our family focus. The culture we were dealing with was preventing our families from ever being around the dinner table or at home together on the same night. We felt that if they had a night set aside to go to church, then we wanted to sacrifice that for them to be the family.

We challenged each family to set aside one night and declare it holy. By this I mean that nothing could touch it and that it would be set apart at the sacrifice of all else. We asked our families to share a meal together (around a table, not a TV) and to engage in fun but also spiritual conversations or activities. We knew that in order for them to take this huge step of putting the primary midweek program in their homes, we would need to support them with training and resources.

The resource came first. We created a magazine-style book-let called *HomeFront* that included recipes, traditions, creative activities, worship, storytelling, time in God's Word, prayer, and conversation starters. Each issue focused on one of the ten environments outlined in my book *Spiritual Parenting* (see appendix A of this book). In each issue, families were able to "create their own adventure" by choosing activities that focused on one of the environments. There was enough to do in each issue that a family could use it for an entire month.

Then came the training. We knew that if we held a Family Night Training, close to no one would show up. So we simply advertised a fun Family Night for all ages. When families arrived, we had stations set up all over the church, representing the different parts of the *HomeFront* resource. They were able to choose their own adventure and go to any station they desired at any time.

It was so rewarding to watch families play games together, make candles, pray, and discuss God's Word. At the end of the evening we gathered together for singing and worship and then let them in on our little secret. We gave each of them a copy of the resource and said, "Look how easy doing a family night is—*you just did it*." With that positive experience and understanding of what it looked like, moms and dads, grandparents and kids all went home planning their next family night together. And the tradition began.

A Family of Families

We all know the adage that it takes a village to raise a child. And when I look at many of the children that our churches are losing, I can't help but wonder if we have lost our village-ness. It's so easy to lead individual lives outside of community. As I look through Scripture it is clear that God never intended it to be this way.

The ever-changing landscape of the family further isolates us. In my latest ministry we had children from two-parent, single parent, blended, broken, gay partner, grandparent, co-parent, and foster homes. Equipping parents to be spiritual leaders in our homes has never been more challenging or diverse.

Today's family ministry needs a mission that says the entire faith community will feel the responsibility of raising a spiritually transformed generation of children—taking into account single people, grandparents, and children who are simply without parents to play that spiritual role. The reality is that many children don't have spiritually supportive parents. But by being part of the larger faith community, these children can still experience authentic, organic, and life-transforming spiritual guidance from loving adults in the church community.

Broadening our understanding of "parenting" and creating intergenerational activities are two ways we can facilitate this. Any class, serving opportunity, mission trip, or family event/service can include the option to bring along a mentor, a grandparent, a co-parent, an uncle or aunt, or even a friend's parent. As we help our families think outside the box about what it means to be "family," they will be less likely to exclude themselves and think their situation is less than perfect. Let's face it—every one of us has a family situation that is less than perfect.

Reflections on Parenting

I recently had the opportunity to take a six-hour drive with my eighteen-year-old son—just him and me. While driving, I asked him if I could interview him about the way his father and I had raised him. I asked, "What kinds of things formed your faith and have had a lasting impact on you?"

Family Night

The first thing he said was, "When I look back on our home life together, one of the things I wouldn't change is the time we set aside every week to do a family night." That wasn't what I thought he would say. We put a lot of emphasis on family night, but I confess to you that as a parent, it was the single most difficult thing I fought for. There were scheduling conflicts, bad attitudes, friends, homework, fatigue, lack of interest, and just plain old laziness.

Of course, when your kids are little, every night is family night. You're all around the dinner table, and they're eating their carrots and their applesauce, and it's hard to imagine that life will ever be different. But when your children get older, slowly but surely they're missing a few nights at dinner, and unless you are tenaciously intentional and claim that territory, there will seldom be time around the family dinner table.

The Red Plate

When my son was a year old and my daughter was three, we lived in a neighborhood with a lot of high schoolers. I'd be cooking dinner, and suddenly all the high school students would show up at my house. So I started making large pots of spaghetti and lots of pizzas because I knew they were coming over. One evening I was tired, and I looked at this group of teenagers sitting in my house, and I asked, "Don't you have homes to go to? Do your parents not feed you? You're always here."

I was just trying to be funny, but some of them said, "No, not really. My family never has dinner together. I never see my parents. I don't remember, other than Christmas or Thanksgiving, sitting down and having dinner together." It gave me a glimpse forward. We get stuck in the day to day. In parenting (especially when the kids are little), the days are long—but ultimately the years are short. I realized that even though my one- and three-year-old were at the dinner table every night, that wouldn't always be the case. So we set aside the sacred day. Sometimes it was Monday night, sometimes it was Sunday night, sometimes it was Friday night, depending on sports schedules or whatever else was happening. But we declared one night a week to be family night.

My son remembered the kinds of conversations we had and the things we did at that dinner table. Every family night, I took out our red plate that said *You are special today*. This was a tradition in our family. We would think of somebody to affirm for something that had happened that week, and they would get the red plate.

Endings and Beginnings

My husband and I recently moved away from our home, five hours from our college-aged children. (I've now become an empty nester, reflective on the season that I have recently completed.) We moved on a Saturday, and Sunday night had traditionally held the place as our family night. That first Sunday night, I sat in my new house, sulking. I thought, "It's family night, but we're *not doing it*. After twenty years of family night, now it's over." I was mourning it.

So I got on Facebook and pulled up my son's page, and there was a picture of him I'll never forget! He and his friends were sitting around our dining room table, and the caption read *family night*. And everybody had a red plate! He had bought red plastic plates for not just one person, but everyone. He later told me he gave a word of affirmation to each of them. He said, "I just made spaghetti, salad, and garlic bread, and we did family night. None of my friends ever had family night, and I wanted to pass on what we had to them." So the tradition of family night lives on. I'm glad I didn't give up—I really am.

On Mission

The second thing my son remembered our family doing that deeply affected him were the times we had carved out to go on mission together. Sometimes that was locally, but very often it was globally. He remembered the times when he got to put his faith into practice, when he was outside the comfort zone of the food he normally ate and the bed he normally slept in and the language he normally spoke, and he was doing things he normally wouldn't do.

Things like being in dramas and puppet shows or doing VBS when he was only in second grade himself. Those opportunities allowed him to stretch his faith muscles and to see a world that was different from our small life in southern California. Those experiences are forever imprinted on him, the acts of service and the times when he was out of his comfort zone, learning to depend on God's Spirit. Now that he is older, he has chosen his own mission fields, whether working on a farm in Portland or ministering abroad to the youth in El Salvador.

It reminded me that while our Christian lives as children can be so much about what we are *learning* about God, we need to give opportunities for children to *play out* those learnings in everyday life—putting their faith into action (more about this in chapter 6).

Modeling

The third thing he mentioned was watching my husband and me. He was an eyewitness to the fact that we didn't live perfect lives, but he saw us attempting to live out the things we said we believed. Not perfectly, but also not just on Sundays. He said, "It's true how much as kids we really watched you. And those things you modeled for us, those are ingrained in me more than anything else."

My son attended a Christian school from kindergarten through eighth grade. Then he went into the public high school system. That's a traumatizing time for families and for students. Both of my children were seduced by things of the world during high school. Nobody's immune from it, and my children bear the marks. A lot of it had to do with the people they were around, but some of it just has to do with figuring out faith in a fallen world. Both of my kids have always been very attracted to lost people. On a really good day I'm so proud of them, and on a bad day I think, "Why do you want to hang out with these people?" It's hard, as parents, to feel out of control of the spiritual development of our children, isn't it?

Translating Grace

One morning, shortly after my son started high school, there was a note from him lying in front of my bedroom door when I woke up. It said, "Mom and Dad, last night three people could not go home, and they needed a place to sleep. I didn't know what to do, but then I remembered that one time you said Jesus washed the feet of sinners, so I let them sleep in the corner. I hope it's okay. Love, Brendon."

I love that he was so *gracious* to let them sleep *in the corner*. I'm not sure exactly where that was in our house. And I don't remember saying Jesus washed the feet of sinners. But somehow, in a moment when he had to choose to extend grace and love or judgment and shame, he chose grace. And he did it based on something we had said or done, evidently.

That's how important modeling is. Parents don't always have to get it right, because the beauty is that when we get it wrong, we just say, "I got that wrong. That didn't reflect our heavenly Father." We get to redeem all of it.

We're so far from perfect parents. Our kids are so far from having their spiritual lives all together. We are such an average family in that regard, just desperately going after faith in the messiness of it all. But my son's words during that drive were very insightful to me. I left that conversation feeling more impassioned than ever about the need to help parents create places where faith can be formed in everyday conversations, just as Deuteronomy 6 commissions us to do. Places where faith can be formed, places where faith can be put into action, and places where faith can be modeled in the good and the bad.

Who Not What

Mark DeVries said in his book *Family-Based Youth Ministry*:

> Almost without exception, those young people who are growing in their faith as adults were teenagers who fit into one of two categories: either (1) they

came from families where Christian growth was modeled in at least one of their parents, or (2) they had developed significant connections with an extended family of adults within the church. How often they attended youth events (including Sunday school and discipleship groups) was not a good predictor of which teens would, and which would not, grow toward Christian adulthood.[3]

These words are probably something we know intuitively. If we look back on our own transformation, there is probably a name, a person, associated with that. Yet we find ourselves busy with getting kids to events and programs, making sure they "know" all the right stuff. We can never underestimate the power of allowing our kids to be in relationship with mentors and parents who are themselves pursuing God with passion and commitment.

After my son and I finished our conversation, I told him, "You know, this stuff will preach!" These examples are in essence a place for families to create a space for *faith to be formed* (our family nights), *faith in action* (on mission), and *faith modeled* (in our home, by our lives). How will you lead your families to consider faith formed, put into action, and modeled? How is God prompting you to respond to spiritual formation in the home?

MINISTRY ASSESSMENT

We have looked at a variety of ways to make parents the primary leaders in their homes—how to come alongside them in supportive ways, and how to rely upon God's Spirit to transform as He chooses.

Take some time to consider the ways that God is prompting you to respond right now.

Reflect

Think back to the four models of family ministry. Which one might be a good starting point for your church? How can you come alongside parents to inspire or equip them to think through how they can instill faith that will last past the years when their children are in their homes? Write down one thing that you can do as an action step. It might be to get a book. It might be to call a friend. It might be to set a date for some training. It might be to simply set aside some time to pray. But choose an action step that you can do today or this week that will help you come alongside your parents in practical ways for faith development.

Respond

Take some time to respond to God, based on the things that He has revealed to you. In what areas will you need humility? Courage or boldness? How will your response reveal where your faith is today? In what ways can you support your parents this week or month? What is one tangible thing you can do today?

Dream

What dreams might God be dreaming for you? What dreams do you have for your faith community or the homes you have been given influence over? How might God be fanning your flame today to take a courageous step of faith to make that dream a reality?

4

FAITH IN FORMATION

....

The Transforming Power of Christ

[The] ability to be honest about ... desolation
[brings us] to the end of [our] self-reliance, which
in turn open[s] up space for God to be at work.
Ruth Haley Barton, Strengthening the Soul of Your Leadership

What comes to mind when you think of spiritual formation? The first time I heard this phrase, I was in my early twenties and working as a leader in children's ministry. The *really* spiritual women of our church were going away on a "spiritual formation" retreat. These women were the ones we all revered. They seemed to have an aura of holiness around them whenever they walked into a room. I wondered how they got that way. So I asked one of them, "What is it that you actually do on a spiritual formation retreat, anyway?"

This person said, "Well, you see, there is fasting and prayer … and lots of solitude and contemplation."

That didn't sound like any women's retreat I had ever been on. Women's retreats typically involved an abundance of yummy food, lots of socialization, and well, of course, prayer. But I got the impression that spiritual formation was for the holiest of holy people. The really, really special people did *those* things.

Christ Formed in You

But it turns out that I was wrong. I now know better. I believe all of our families need spiritual formation. Parents need it. Children need it. But it's not in a formulaic package of ingredients. It's not necessarily defined by what we do or don't do. Rather, it depends upon what Christ is doing in us.

Recall Paul's words in Galatians 4:19: "My dear children, for whom I am again in the pains of childbirth until *Christ is formed in you*." Paul was saying to the spiritually young Galatian church, "I long for the day when Christ is formed in you." He longed for this as a mother in labor would long for the birth of her child. He realized that all had been accomplished to allow this to happen. The time was the here and now. And like Paul, I find myself longing for the day when Christ is formed in our families.

Paul sent a similar message to the church in Corinth when he wrote, "Though our outer self is wasting away, our inner self is being renewed day by day" (2 Cor. 4:16 ESV). I have reached the age when I'm well aware that my outer self is wasting away. But in contrast, I want the daily renewal of the *inner self* for me … and for the children and parents in this generation.

Paul went on to contrast the temporal things with those that are eternal, death with life, and the seen versus the unseen. These things that are unseen, that are eternal, that are not of this world—these are the things the Holy Spirit is renewing in us because of the Father's great love and because of what Christ did on the cross. That's spiritual formation. That's Christ formed in you.

So maybe you're on board with the idea of family ministry. Maybe you've bought into including parents as integral to the process. But before we launch into how to craft this type of ministry and how to train our volunteers, we need to be clear on the goal. Family ministry *for what*? We love parents. But creating a ministry around parents is a lot more work and far riskier than merely ministering to kids, so we need to have a clear motivation for doing it. I suggest that this is the goal:

CHRIST FORMED IN YOU

Dreaming of More

I'm dreaming of more. I want more for this generation than the generation that preceded it. I want more for this generation than the generation I grew up in. I want more of God in my life, and I want more of God for my children, for my grandchildren, and for the families in my ministry. I want more!

Todd Proctor from ROCKHARBOR Church said, "God dreams bigger for us than we could ever dream for ourselves." This is so true, isn't it? God dreams for the children and families entrusted to you. And God dreams for you, His child, more than you can imagine. If we put ourselves in proximity to that dream, we will be changed.

When we think about the families in our ministries or the children in our homes, do we have a growing discomfort to see *Christ formed in you*? Do we long for the day when Christ will be formed in each one of them? If not, our first step is to beg God to put that yearning in our hearts, first for ourselves and then for those in our care.

Three Temptations

I believe, however, that as this discomfort grows among us as parents and ministry leaders, we are at risk of what family pastor and leader in spiritual formation Kit Rae calls falling into one of three great temptations. After years of dreaming or hard work in our ministries, if we don't see the results that we hoped to have, we may become vulnerable to temptation. If we don't see Christ formed in the lives of others in the way that satisfies us, we're tempted to make our ministries about *something else*.

Temptation 1: Communicate Information without Formation

First, we're tempted to make our ministries about information, facts, head knowledge, and things that we can measure. If children and families learn information, we may be tempted to pat ourselves on the back for training them in the faith. But maybe we shouldn't. Children may memorize Bible verses. They may know how many stones David used to kill Goliath. It's good, but it's *not enough*.

When I was in my graduate studies and preparing to write my dissertation, one of my professors said, "You have two options. You can make your dissertation an empirical study or a longitudinal study." An empirical study is one that is measured in mathematical terms. We create a survey of some kind, and the respondent chooses yes or no; true or false; a, b, c, or d. We can then run the data through a mathematical statistical analysis, and we come up with the facts. It's objective.

By contrast, a longitudinal study can be more subjective. It happens over time. The Fuller Institute recently published a book entitled *Sticky Faith*. This research study measured six hundred kids over a period of six years. Their findings have continued to fuel the fire for parents to assume their roles as spiritual leaders in their children's lives. However this was a longitudinal study that sought to assess things over time and did so in more subjective ways.

A mentor relationship or a parent relationship is subjective. We're hands-on eyewitnesses to a person's life. This is not something we can measure statistically. We can't measure the effect of mentoring in an hour of Sunday school or church. We can't measure it at the end of the quarter or even at the time children leave our ministry and enter middle school, high school, or college. But I believe the longitudinal study is the eternal perspective that Paul called us to in 2 Corinthians: "So we fix our eyes not on what is seen, but on what is unseen, since what is seen is temporary, but what is unseen is eternal" (4:18). He wanted our ministries to focus on the things that are unseen, the things that are eternal.

What would it look like for us to have eyes that look more broadly than the hour on a Sunday morning? More broadly than one year or even the time in our ministries? To have those eyes, eternal eyes, we need to avoid the temptation of settling for just information.

Temptation 2: Make Ministry about Moral Training

The second temptation is that we can make our ministries about moral training, good behavior, or "how to look like a Christian in ten easy steps." This has been tempting for me as a parent, because good behavior looks so much like faith on the outside. The children look well-mannered, they go to church, they bring their Bibles, they memorize their verses, they say they're sorry when they've hurt someone, they may go on mission trips, they may give some of their money as an offering, and they participate in selfless acts of kindness. When we've taught them those things, it's tempting for us to say to ourselves, "Good job! Look how *spiritual* my child is!"

Certainly when children are young, moral behavior is indeed what we teach them. We have to tell them, "Say thank you. Don't hit your brother. Tell the truth." We don't converse with them about this; these are the rules. In the moment of teaching these things, we almost don't even care about their hearts, because these are just things you do to live in this world in proximity to other people.

But as our children grow up, we as leaders and parents often don't grow with them. I see this temptation in myself: I may have a fifteen-year-old son, and I'm still saying, "Don't do drugs. Don't have sex with your girlfriend. Say you're sorry. Don't hit your sister." When we do this, we continue to use moral behavior tactics at the stage when moral development needs to be transcended by spiritual development. In spiritual development the child's heart is what matters … not just the actions. This is the stage when we need to let the Holy Spirit come in and act in that child's life. Yet if we don't make that transition, we fall into the temptation of making our ministries (and our homes) about just being a really *good person*. But really good people are not what Jesus asked for. He asked for people of faith. And faith is so much messier (and harder to measure) than moral behavior.

Temptation 3: Despair

The third temptation is to simply despair. To give up. Sometimes we look at our churches, at our families, at the leadership above us, and we feel unappreciated. We feel criticized. We feel discouraged. One of the Enemy's greatest tactics is to discourage ministry leaders and parents. As I travel the country, I can't tell you how many discouraged ministers and parents I meet. There's a strong temptation to despair and give up.

Kit Rae offers this insight:

> Often we despair in the very process itself because we don't see transformation happening. We wonder where God has gone. We wonder why we don't see faith like we want to see it or how others see it in their ministries. We don't see God working and so we lose the "through line" and begin to make our ministries about *other* things, buildings, decor, volunteer training, or leadership development. In addition I think we even stop seeing transformation in our own lives and we despair. We fake it and continue in a posture that is nothing but a fabrication … but what we truly long for is something *real*, for God to show up![1]

People are leaving ministry in unprecedented numbers. And they would probably leave parenting if they could. But what's even worse is when we "leave"—but we stay in. Think of the times when we've "left" ministry, but we still show up to work every day. Think of the times when we've left mothering or fathering, but we still show up. Mentally, emotionally, and spiritually, we've left. That's a problem.

So we are at a point where we need to make a decision about spiritual formation not only for our own lives, but for the sake of families. Because the reality is that we are going to be tempted by these three things. The first step is simply to acknowledge these temptations, to give them language, because we disarm them a bit when we're aware.

By Definition

The next step in resisting those temptations is to unpack that phrase in Galatians 4:19: *Christ formed in you.* We don't need some high and lofty explanation of spiritual formation that only the really smart or really spiritual will understand. We all need to understand *Christ formed in you.* We need to be able to wake up every day in our families and in our ministry context and say, *Christ formed in you.* Let's look at each of these concepts separately: Christ, Formed, in You.

Christ

Let's take the first word first: *Christ.* Christ is central to the gospel, right? He is the gospel. He is the good news. Paul addressed this in Colossians 1:15–23. I'm overwhelmed with the power of the words he chose. The power that rests in this proclamation that Christ is preeminent over all. Listen to the richness of these words: *all things, heaven and earth, the fullness of God.* He is *the One,* the *firstborn from the dead,* the *resurrected one.* He is the *gospel* that is proclaimed. He's *central.* A. W. Tozer once said, "It is either all of Christ or none of Christ! I believe we need to preach again a whole Christ to the world—a Christ who does not need our apologies, a Christ who will not be divided, a Christ who will either be Lord of all or will not be Lord at all!"[2] When we think about spiritual formation, we can't have *Christ formed in you* without Christ being central. And yet I still find myself allowing other things to become supreme over Christ in my ministry.

The Center of the Gospel

One of my favorite books in the Bible is the book of Hebrews. It is a compelling argument set out to defend the legitimacy of Christ and the new covenant. Writing to Hebrews who were new converts to the Christian faith, the author placed Christ as superior to all other institutions and people that Jewish culture held dear:

- Chapter 1: Jesus is greater than the angels
- Chapter 2: Jesus is greater than any man
- Chapter 3: Jesus is greater than Moses
- Chapter 4: Jesus is greater than the Sabbath
- Chapter 5: Jesus is greater than the priesthood
- Chapter 6: Jesus is greater than Abraham
- Chapter 7: Jesus is greater than the high priest
- Chapter 8: Jesus is greater than the tabernacle
- Chapter 9: Jesus is greater than the law
- Chapter 10: Jesus is greater than the sacrificial system

After this airtight defense, the author began to tell the original Big God Story, recounting individuals throughout biblical history who by faith chose the greater thing. All of these were the pillars of the Old Testament community. In fact, the priesthood, the law, the tabernacle, and so on were the very things God gave them. Yet even good things, given to us by God, can take false primacy in our lives and ministries if we're not watchful.

Hebrews 11 is this account and is not only a historical overview but also a captivating narrative of men and women of whom the "world was not worthy" (v. 38). As chapter 12 opens, the readers are charged to take note of this "great cloud of witnesses" (v. 1), all of whom kept their eyes focused on the goal. We as New Testament believers are charged to take note of these living testaments of faith and keep our eyes focused on Jesus, the author and perfecter of our faith.

The author could have ended this discourse after chapter 10 because certainly the point of Christ's supremacy had been made. Yet the author also understood the power of story and that this story was still being written. The encouragement given in chapters 11–13 is a rally cry for inspiration and hope. It's a coach's call to his athletes in the locker room at halftime to not give up!

When I read Hebrews, I wonder what this author would say about our ministries today. What things have we made more central to the gospel than Jesus? Is it our buildings, our staff, our worship, our programs, or our curriculum? How can we go back to the centrality of the gospel, and the centrality of the story, making Jesus the center of all we do? After all, any other message we offer will not transform.

With Jesus?

I greatly admire Scottie May, a professor at Wheaton College and a prolific author on children's spirituality and faith formation. When I first met her, I could barely speak, I was so nervous. I was starting to be awakened to some of the things that she was in strong support of, and she said she'd come to visit my ministry. I was anxious as she walked around observing my ministry. I couldn't read her face. At the end she asked me a question that I know she had asked countless people before me. She said, "Michelle, this is so great. I love what you've done. It's fun, it's relevant, it's exciting, and it's excellent. You've done such a great job. But when do the children get to *be with* Jesus?"

My heart sank. And her words made me slightly defensive. Hadn't she seen the kids saying their Bible verse? That was about Jesus. And wasn't she listening during the teaching time, when Jesus was walking on the water? That was about Jesus. And our craft was a picture of Jesus. We even sang songs about Jesus. So what was she talking about? But her question was different. When do your children get to *be with* Jesus? When do they have a chance to pause, be still, and listen to Him? When can they have a taste of silence from the busy world to talk to Him, speak to Him, and sit with Him in concern or celebration? Her question has altered forever the way that I minister to children.

We need to make Him central, the focus of all we do. We need to resist getting distracted by doing things *about* Him and instead create an environment where children encounter Him. How do we create an environment for kids to hear God's voice and just be with Him? What might possibly happen in our midst when we commit ourselves to do that?

Formed

So in order for formation to take place, we have established that Christ must have primacy. He is to be lifted up and acknowledged in all things. No program, Bible narrative, or activity can be worthy of our time and energy if it doesn't move our focus back to Him. Now let's look at the word *formed.* What does it mean to be formed?

Information and Transformation

As we saw earlier, one of the mistakes we can make about spiritual formation is to confuse it with information. We think if we can get children to memorize the facts and figures and hide the words of the Bible in their hearts, then when they're older and no longer in our homes and ministries, they'll have faith. Now, helping children hide the Word in their hearts is a beautiful passion. Every one of us should have that passion. But if children learn information exclusively, then that alone is not transformative.

Think about the narrative of Noah and the flood. How many days and nights did it rain? Our children know: forty. How many of each type of animal were on the ark? Most of our children will learn that there were two of each, and a few will remember that for some species there were seven. And what kind of wood was the ark made of? Yes, it was gopher wood. I've never seen gopher wood, but somehow we all know this fact. However, I've never been in a service where people were giving their testimonies of a transformed life—and somebody walked up to a microphone and said, "I just want to say that it was that *gopher wood* that changed my life."

In and of themselves none of these things matter. They are a foundation for something else. And that something else is this formational piece. Formation is where kids meet with Jesus; they're hearing from Him; they're sitting in solitude and silence. We don't often think of kids sitting in solitude and silence, but they can. And God speaks to them. This is an important part of how we're formed. Spiritual formation is not just when somebody else tells us something, but when God tells it to us or we feel His conviction.

It's in those quiet places where He's formed within us through genuine relationship. The information is part of the fertilizer that allows the formation to take root. Too often we make our ministries about either/or instead of both/and. Yet it's in the marriage of the information and the formation that we have transformation. We need to marry those two things and remind ourselves that the soul learns differently than the mind does. We have to capture both with intentionality.

Ready to Live

Dallas Willard, a philosopher and author in the field of spiritual formation, said this in his book *The Great Omission:*

> We have counted on preaching, teaching, and knowledge or information to form faith in the hearer, and have counted on faith to form the inner life and outward behavior of the Christian. But, for whatever reason, this strategy has not turned out well. The result is that we have multitudes of professing Christians who well may be ready to die but obviously are not ready to live, and can hardly get along with themselves, much less with others.[3]

Wow. That's a really strong statement about the condition of our Christian world today. But without formation, that's what happens. If it's just information, we may be ready to die because we've made a profession of Christ as Lord and Savior. But what about the life that He gave us here? What about John 10:10, where Jesus said He came to give us life and to give it to us abundantly? He's come to give us life, here and *now*. What about that? What about living for our faith, not just dying for our faith? I'd like to think that we are committed as ministry leaders and parents to taking rich truth, which this generation so desperately needs, and offering it in a place of formation. I dream that we will create environments that offer information and formation together.

Three Goals

The church's educational focus over the past seven decades has tended to enhance these three things:

> *External listening*—gaining knowledge through books, teachers, and resources
> *Obedience*—behavioral change
> *Trying harder*—if you disobey, you need to strive to get better

By contrast, if we aim toward the transformation of the soul, we will aim at these:

> *Internal listening*—learning to discern God's voice
> *Desiring to obey*—wanting to follow God's voice

> *Obeying in the power of the Holy Spirit*—recognizing that
> it's less about trying harder and more about learning to
> abide in Christ while relying on the Spirit's power for
> transformation

Let's take these three goals one at a time. First, we desire that children and families would be able to hear God's voice. That they'd discern it over all the other voices clamoring for their attention. Of course, God doesn't necessarily speak the same way to each person. He may speak one way to me and another way to you.

But what I've learned is that He speaks to each of us consistently, as a father would speak, so that we can learn to trust that consistent voice. And we can shepherd children to help them discern how God speaks to *them* and lean into *that* voice. We can also help them understand that we all go through times when we can't hear God's voice, and that's okay, because He's still speaking. He's still alive. That's where faith comes in: trusting Him when He speaks, and trusting Him when He seems silent.

So first, we want to create an environment in which children and families will learn to hear God's voice and will know it's His. Second, we want an environment in which when they hear God's voice, they will desire to obey it. We can't make them obey it, but we can create an environment that encourages them to desire to obey it. We won't ask them to simply emulate rote behavior, because we want them to desire to obey out of a relationship. We will need to model what it means to be in relationship with God.

And third, we want them to know how to obey in the power of God's Spirit. We don't want them just trying to obey, mustering up the will power and *trying harder*. For whatever reason, many people heard this as their three-point sermon growing up: "God is good—You are bad—Try harder!" But this is not the entire story. Of course God is good, and we know we have all sinned … but the remedy is not to try harder; the remedy is to be encouraged and trained to abide in Christ and the power of His Spirit for transformation.

It's a lifetime journey to learn to abide in Christ, isn't it? Just when I think I've been abiding, I don't even know what it means anymore. Or I do it in one circumstance, and then I feel like a failure in another circumstance. This is a lifelong faith muscle that God is developing in us, teaching us to submit to Him, and our children are on exactly the same journey with us.

For as challenging as it sometimes feels to abide in Christ, unless each of us chooses to obey in the power of the Holy Spirit, we will fail in the Christian life. Over and over, college students and twenty-somethings tell me, "That Christianity thing didn't work for me." And when I unpack what they're saying, I think, "Of course it didn't work." How in the world can we ever live out the words in the Bible unless we are empowered?

When Jesus was leaving with the promise of the Spirit, He told His disciples not to leave Jerusalem. I can almost hear Him saying, "Don't you *dare* leave Jerusalem. You're going to be in really big trouble. Don't you dare leave, because until the Spirit comes, you won't *be able* to do the things I've trained you to do." In the same way, unless our children and families wait on Christ and learn to work with the Spirit, they won't truly be transformed. The Christianity thing won't work for them. It won't work for us either.

A Hidden Heart

To understand the crucial place the Holy Spirit has in transforming us as we abide in Christ, it's important to look at the condition of our hearts. John Coe, director of spiritual formation at Talbot School of Theology, once said, "We are in danger of creating a 'hidden heart' very early in life. But it is when we see the true condition of our hearts that we recognize our need to depend upon God's Spirit to transform us and not simply fake spirituality."[4] As we shepherd children's hearts, we have to be aware of the way sin has marred the heart of every person since the fall. In Genesis 3 we read:

> When the woman saw that the fruit of the tree was good for food and pleasing to the eye, and also desirable for gaining wisdom, she took some and ate it. She also gave some to her husband, who was with her, and he ate it. Then the eyes of both of them were opened, and they realized they were naked; so they sewed fig leaves together and made coverings for themselves.
>
> Then the man and his wife heard the sound of the LORD God as he was walking in the garden in the cool of the day, and they hid from the LORD God among the trees of the garden. But the LORD God called to the man, "Where are you?"
>
> He answered, "I heard you in the garden, and I was afraid because I was naked; so I hid." (vv. 6–10)

These sobering words inform our ministry. After the first man and woman sinned, their eyes were opened, and they realized they were naked. So they sewed fig leaves together to cover themselves. And when they heard the Lord nearby, they *hid* from Him. When the Lord called to the man, he said he was afraid because he was naked, so he hid. In other words, as soon as the man and woman sinned, they understood shame. Shame led to guilt, and guilt led to hiding.

It's essential that we understand this path. So many parents have called me and said, "My child is lying. My child is hiding their sin, and I'm shocked and appalled." Yet we do the same thing. I'm a professional hider of sin. At our core, we're all professionals at this. Sin enters our human heart, and we feel shame and guilt, and we're deeply resistant to facing that squarely, so we hide.

From Hiding to Healing

Our ministries and homes need to be places where kids can come out of hiding. In the garden, God called to Adam and Eve. He sought them out and called to them and invited them out of hiding. And even when they refused to fully come clean, He acted in love toward them. In the first sacrifice of a life, He sewed together animal skins for them, because where there is sin, there is death. And as the cross shows us, where there is sin and death, there is the offer of forgiveness. When sin comes out of hiding, it can be *healed*.

Hebrews tells us,

> No discipline seems pleasant at the time, but painful. Later on, however, it produces a harvest of

righteousness and peace for those who have been
trained by it.

Therefore, strengthen your feeble arms and
weak knees. "Make level paths for your feet," so that
the lame may not be disabled, but rather healed.
(12:11–13)

Discipline, the author of Hebrews wrote, is for the sake of healing. When our children come out of hiding, there will be healing.
But until we recognize the depravity that each one of us has inside,
this bent toward hiding, we won't be able to nurture an environment
that invites children out of hiding. We'll be constantly shocked by
their sin, and that reaction will only deepen their shame and drive
them further into hiding. They know there's something fundamentally wrong with them. We need to let them know we understand
that and can deal with it.

My Hiding Story

When I was in the eighth grade, I was invited to a New Year's Eve
all-nighter at a girlfriend's church. We were going to bowl and play
broom hockey and have lots of fun, bringing in the new year of
1981. It was an epic event for a fourteen-year-old: over four hundred
middle schoolers staying out all night without curfew. But I had also
been invited to a high school party where there would be high school
boys, some of whom I was very fond of.

After considering both of my options, I chose to go to the high
school party. And in my sinfulness I lied to my parents. I said I
was going to my girlfriend's church for the all-nighter, but when

I got dropped off at the church, I just signed in my name, looked around at four hundred kids, and was sure they would never miss me. So I got into a car and went to the other party with the high school boys.

The party was great fun, and without incident I was dropped off back at the church around five thirty or six o'clock in the morning right when the donuts came out. I assimilated into the herd of students as if I had been there all along. But a feeling of shame was creeping up inside me. And then I had a twinge of guilt. One of the leaders came up to me and said, "Michelle, where have you been all night?"

I said, "Oh, I was here. I was on those buses, maybe you didn't see me, but I was here. I bowled a … uh, uh, 290, yeah, 290, that's it." I hid. The lie came to my tongue because the shame and guilt inside me made me want to hide.

Then another leader came up to me, and another friend, and I thought, *Hey everybody, back off.* Did I have a sign on me telling everyone what I had done? It felt like *everybody* knew my sin. I had to keep covering and making more lies upon more lies. Finally somebody started drilling down on the fact that I wasn't on a bus when they did roll call. So instead of coming out of hiding, I told yet another lie. Now consider the stupidity of my next statement, "Actually, my grandma got really sick in the middle of the night, and my dad came and picked me up to take me to see her. But then he dropped me off again."

When you're fourteen, that sounds like a reasonable story. I wish I could have heard the thoughts in the leader's head that night: *Okay, sure, that's credible. Right.*

When my mom and dad picked me up and asked how the night went, I told more lies. I was hating life by now, but I was too deep in it to turn back. With that much lying, how could I ever come clean? So I just lived with the guilt and what Dallas Willard said is the full-time job of *sin management.* That much lying and hiding is a full-time job! How can we ever have life abundant when we're managing our sin like that?

Weeks went by. (It may have been days, but it felt like weeks.) Finally my friend's dad decided to do the right thing and cleverly called my mom and said, "We're *concerned* about Michelle's grandmother and her health."

Mom said, "Grandma walked five miles this morning. Whatever are you referring to?"

My friend's dad said, "Oh. We were just concerned because on New Year's Eve Michelle had to leave the party because your husband picked her up to visit her sick grandmother." (Insert ominous music here.)

You can imagine the look on my mom's face. I was sitting there, watching her hang up the phone. I knew instantly that I was going to be grounded for life.

I'd been raised in the church. I'd memorized Bible verses. I was a leader in middle school ministry. I was even at a Christian school. My parents were in leadership at the church. My dad was the head elder. So I had all the "right stuff" around me. And I knew truth. But when we're tempted and we sin, we have shame and guilt, and we hide. Some of us will go to extraordinary efforts to not be found out. God knows that. And *we* need to know it … for the children and families in our ministries. We need to be able to say, "You're like me, and we're like Adam and Eve, and that's what we do—we hide. But we can come out of hiding."

That day, God chose to bring me out of hiding. My parents dealt with not only the issue at hand, but with my deeper issue, the issue of sin and shame.

Three Perceptions

Children will come out of hiding only if they feel safe. Therefore, we desperately need God to help us create environments in which people *feel safe* to come out. As we create such environments, we need to address possible perceptions people may have, because these perceptions radically affect the way their hearts are formed. Another way to think of this is that this is our *unconscious theology*—these are the things that drive and dictate our behaviors regardless of what we say or hear. And the level at which we are *unaware* of these perceptions/theologies is the level at which we are not truly in control of our behaviors. The perceptions to be aware of are:

> Perception of commitment to God
> Perception of relationship with God
> Perception of God and His character

Perception of Commitment

First, what is this person's perception of commitment to God? Commitment is crucial in the Christian faith. Does commitment mean, "I prayed a onetime prayer, I asked Jesus into my heart at VBS or Sunday school or in the car, and now I'm good to go"? If that's my perception of commitment, then I'm going to live my life of *Christ formed in you* in a distorted way. That view of commitment is for when I die someday; it's for getting rid of sin and being able to go to heaven, but that's a long time from now.

Some people perceive commitment like this—as just praying a prayer. But in Mark 8:34, Jesus said commitment is something totally different. He said, "Whoever wants to be my disciple must deny themselves and take up their cross and follow me." It's a lifelong journey. Do we paint commitment that way in our ministries? Do we paint it that way in our homes? Do we tell our children that this will be a lifelong journey where they will die to themselves every single day because their lives are no longer their own?

In Galatians 2:20 Paul said, "I have been crucified with Christ and I no longer live." Do we think this is our life? This is not our life. As believers in Christ by faith, we've given it up. We've surrendered all rights and privileges to our former life. Paul continued, "I no longer live, but Christ lives in me. The life I now live in the body, I live by faith in the Son of God, who loved me and gave himself for me." That perception of commitment is miles away from a life of hiding and sin management. We need to help children and families recognize the difference, and we need to model for them what it's like to live this way.

Perception of Relationship

Second, what is this person's perception of relationship? When we're talking to a child or his or her parent or a leader, we need to remember that they have a perception of their relationship with God. Do they see Him as their BFF? Is Jesus their best friend? If so, what does that mean? At any given point, a best friend can be wonderful or the worst thing in our life. Sometimes our friends let us get away with unthinkable things because they've got our back—they understand. Is Jesus really just a friend, or is He Other? Is He magnificently *Other*?

A child or a parent might have the perception that God is Father. We know the connotations that come with that: warm and loving, or abusive, or abandoning. Who is the child's natural father? This is one reason why family ministry is so important. Do we understand our children in the context of their family? Do they have a father? Who is their father? What's the nature of their father? What happens behind closed doors? *Father* is a loaded term. Or is God a boss? Is He a judge? All of these perceptions play into how a person will be formed both by life experiences and the things they are taught.

We also need to explore how people perceive God blessing them in this relationship. Do they think of blessing as just the good things? For instance, our friend's wife gets a job or a new car, or their child gets into a great college, and we say, "Oh, you're so blessed." But what did Jesus say? "Blessed are you when people insult you, persecute you and falsely say all kinds of evil against you because of me" (Matt. 5:11). Blessed are you when you're meek and weak. Yet we don't go up to each other when we're in the time of crisis and say, "You're blessed." We probably wouldn't appreciate it. But we *are* blessed because of God's grace and love in the midst of it. We are never alone. So how do we perceive a relationship in which there is blessing? A person who's under enormous amounts of trial all the time may feel, "God doesn't love me. I'm not His favorite. His favorite is that guy over there."

And how do we perceive the conditions under which God blesses us? Does He bless us when we're good, when we behave ourselves? Or is His blessing abundant simply because of Christ? I was recently talking to a gentleman in his fifties. He had been raised in Sunday school, but in his early twenties he had walked deliberately away from God and into a very sinful life. In the last year and a half, though, he had come back to his faith and made enormous changes in his life. I saw so many rich things happening, so I asked, "Do you feel blessed?"

He said, "Yeah, I feel blessed. I mean, now that I've gotten my life together." He took me through the past eighteen months and how he was back at church and giving sacrificially. He said, "I feel blessed by God, because I finally got my act together."

I felt prompted to offer another perspective: "I wonder if the blessing started long before that. I wonder if God was blessing you years or even decades before you saw it, wooing your heart back to Him." Tears rolled down his cheeks at the thought of that. The blessing comes from our Father because He loves us, because of His grace and mercy, not necessarily based on the things that we do or don't do.

Perception of God and His Character

Third, what is this person's perception of God and His character? Who is God? How is it that a good God can allow evil things to happen in this life? How could God send people to hell? What is His character? A person's perception of the constants of God will influence how he or she is formed. Because God is "other" and "greater than" us, we struggle to understand Him and the character that guides His decisions.

Any portion of Scripture can give us fodder to demand that God is one way until we read another passage. Then, perhaps, we are uncertain. This uncertainty can breed distrust or misperceptions. However, we know that God reveals Himself as unchangeable, good, loving, just, merciful, and passionate about being in relationship with each of us. The environments we create for faith formation need to take all of this into account.

In You

So we have discussed Christ in His primacy. And we have considered the elements that affect how a person's heart is formed: hearing God's Spirit and responding, sin and hiding, and our perceptions of Him. Now finally, we have the phrase *in you*. *In you* is the magnificent truth that God went from being faraway and untouchable, where we couldn't even speak His name, to dwelling in the very hearts and lives of those who call Him Lord and Savior. He made us His temple. He has graced us with His presence, and we cannot flee from it. Where can we go where we are away from His Spirit? If we go to the heights, if we go to the depths, He's there. If we are in sin or in confession, where can we go from His Spirit? He is in us. Christ is formed in us through the power of His Spirit.

What does His Spirit do when He's in us? He does what you and I can't do. No matter how great we are as ministers, no matter how eloquent we are as teachers, no matter how fabulous we are as parents, the Holy Spirit forms in each person something we can never do. *He can bring conviction.* It's supernatural.

In Acts 2, when Peter preached after being filled with the Spirit, verse 37 says that when the people heard what he said, "they were cut to the heart." You can cut somebody in the heart with a dagger, and it's destructive. I think that's how we often use guilt, because guilt does often give us the immediate results we want. When you guilt someone into doing something right, you can get an immediate result. But that's not transformation. However, a skilled surgeon with a knife in his or her hand, carving away the impurities around a heart, is cutting to the heart too. But that's for healing and good. That's the Holy Spirit's conviction.

Too often in ministry we use the tactics of guilt and manipulation, because they're available to us *without* the Spirit. In that sense, they seem easier. But if we fall upon Him who is inside us, then He is the One who brings about conviction. In Acts 2, the people were cut to the heart and repented, because conviction leads to true repentance. And they were transformed, because true repentance leads to transformation. So if we want a generation that is transformed, then only the Holy Spirit in us can do that work. Only the Holy Spirit.

MINISTRY ASSESSMENT

Think about this incredibly important thought: God has placed you in a position of influence over a certain amount of people for this time in history. I pray that as God forms His Son in you, then His influence will spill over into the lives and ministries you touch.

Take time to reflect, respond, and dream about how God might want to awaken you to more in your life personally or in your ministry to children and their families.

Reflect

Which of the three temptations are you most vulnerable to? How has that played out in your personal life? In your family? In your ministry? What misperceptions about commitment, relationship, or God Himself have affected your life? How have they affected your ministry?

How would you describe your current approach to family ministry? When did your journey with it begin? How has it shaped you? Borne fruit? How have you seen God bless it? In what ways might it have hindered faith formation in children's or families' lives? Why? What might be disconcerting about laying it down to embrace what God may be doing now?

What might it look like for you to put *Christ formed in you* in the primary place in your ministry? What choices will you need to make in order to do that? What will that require of you? What will it require from others? Spend some time writing an account of your thoughts and reflections.

Respond

Take some time to respond to God based on the things that He has revealed to you. Is this a time of confession or celebration? How will your response reveal where your faith is today? Is this a time for quietness and solitude? Or is this a time for you to have a conversation with a member of your team or a family in your ministry for support or encouragement? However God's Spirit is speaking to you right now, respond to Him in that with a heart of surrender.

Dream

Next, what dreams might God be dreaming for you? Are those dreams desires that can be put into words? Is there a particular next step that you can begin implementing immediately? A person you could share this dream with? How might the things He has revealed to you serve as a catalyst to make some adjustments in your ministry to children and their families? Where can your "ahas" be shared or translated into a ministry opportunity?

WHEN JESUS GAVE US SOMETHING "BETTER"

The Holy Spirit in Motion

> *The truth is that the Spirit of the living God is guaranteed
> to ask you to go somewhere or do something you wouldn't
> normally want or choose to do…. The Holy Spirit of God
> will mold you into the person you were made to be.*
>
> *Francis Chan*, Forgotten God

In his book *Forgotten God*, Francis Chan said this about the modern church's experience with the Holy Spirit:

> I'm willing to bet there are millions of churchgoers across America who cannot confidently say they

have experienced His presence or action in their lives over the past year. And many of them do not believe they can.

The benchmark of success in church services has become more about attendance than the movement of the Holy Spirit. The "entertainment" model of church was largely adopted in the 1980s and '90s, and while it alleviated some of our boredom for a couple of hours a week, it filled our churches with self-focused consumers rather than self-sacrificing servants attuned to the Holy Spirit....

The light of the American church is flickering and nearly extinguished, having largely sold out to the kingdoms and values of this world....

We are not all we were made to be when everything in our lives and churches can be explained apart from the work and presence of the Spirit of God....

Shouldn't there be a huge difference between the person who has the Spirit of God living inside of him or her and the person who does not?[1]

Think about that question for a minute. Shouldn't there be a *huge* difference between those of us who have God's Spirit and those who do not? The answer to us is obvious, but the reality is not as clear.

What is vital, however, is that we live in the truth of a transformed life, not because we *should* but because we *can*—and we *need* to in order to pass on a true faith to the next generation. There is too much at stake to merely scratch our heads and say, "Yeah, that's weird, isn't it?" The children and families in our ministries are looking to us to proclaim the truth of Scripture and the reality of God's power within us. So let's take a look back at our roots, when this journey with God's Spirit began, and what possible implications it could have for our ministry to children and their families.

The Gift Arrives

In Acts 2 we have the account of the day of Pentecost. On this day, the Jewish community from all regions gathered in Jerusalem for the Festival of Harvest (or Pentecost). This festival was celebrated in the summer to mark the harvest of the barley season and occurred fifty days after Passover. Because Jesus had spent forty days with His disciples after His resurrection and was in the grave for three days, this event occurred roughly one week after Jesus's ascension. His instructions were clear, "Remain in Jerusalem until the Spirit comes." So they waited.

Unaware that this would be the occasion that God would choose to pour out His Spirit upon His people, the disciples joined with people from diverse nations and languages to celebrate. God chose to fill the entire place with His Spirit, and His power was among them all. This was the gift that Jesus had said would be better for His disciples than if He stayed among them. While not all the events of that day seem clear to the modern reader, one thing is clear: God's presence changed everything!

Peter spoke with unprecedented boldness. He declared that Jesus is the Messiah, the sacrificed lamb and risen Savior. Over three thousand souls were added to the church that day, and the afterglow of it lasted well beyond the festival. The chapters that follow in the book of Acts show us the holy unity that the early church experienced, giving as each had need and gathering together for fellowship and prayer.

The Spirit of God in Us

The Holy Spirit would now live and dwell among His people for good. He would no longer rest only for a period on those who were anointed for leadership, but within all who would repent of sin and claim Jesus as Savior.

Ephesians tells us that the Holy Spirit is the deposit or down payment of our future inheritance, the mark that we are truly His (1:13–14). In his gospel, John gave language to the Spirit's role in our lives: Counselor, Comforter, Teacher, the One who testifies to all things true (14:12–27). Paul beckoned his readers to walk in step with the Spirit, affirmed His role as our guide (Gal. 5:25), and urged them to not quench or hinder His work through rebellious sin (1 Thess. 5:19; Eph. 4:30).

The Holy Spirit is most often represented as a fire, because He enlightens and awakens the soul and purges, purifies, and refines us. The Spirit is "quenched" when any act is done or word is spoken that is contrary to His character. Someone once observed that fire may be quenched by heaping dirt or water on it, just as the love of the world will grieve and quench the Spirit if we are not vigilant.

Finally, one of the more tender images of the Spirit is in Romans 8, where Paul shared that even when our groanings are too painful or deep for words, the Spirit intercedes for us on our behalf (v. 26).

I'm not sure if we can even imagine a life of faith without the indwelling of the Spirit if we have never known one. Imagine those in the biblical accounts who by faith chose to follow God without the provisions the Spirit gives us. How great is this gift of His Spirit, making us the very temple of His presence? It's astounding, isn't it?

The Holy Spirit and Children

Despite all of this incredible knowledge about God's Spirit and His work to transform us from the inside out, I find that many children's ministries are skeptical about promoting His power and His position. Regardless of denominational differences, we can be confident to teach children from an early age that God's power to live the life to which He calls us is available to them. We can train them to hear His voice, listen to His promptings and tender convictions, and obey His leading by the strength and counseling that He provides. All of these are biblical principles, but much of this first needs to be learned by us as well, wouldn't you agree? I am constantly learning what it means to walk in step with the Spirit and allow Him to lead me.

Chosen Teacher

The Bible says the Holy Spirit is God's chosen teacher; it is He who causes spiritual growth and formation *when* and *as* He chooses. How does this affect *our* role as ministers? While there is nothing wrong with having "Sunday school teachers," it's possible that even that simple title could steal some of what is intended for God alone.

As I mentioned in chapter 2, several years ago we changed the titles of our "teachers" to be "storytellers" or "small group leaders" in order to retain the title of "teacher" for God's Spirit in our ministry. It may seem like we were splitting hairs, but I have realized the power of language in the spiritual development of children, and this was one place where I wanted to be very clear.

So if God's Spirit is teacher, what is *our* role? We can think of our role as creating environments that allow the Holy Spirit to do what He does best: transform lives. Transformation is a supernatural endeavor that only God can do, but we can partner with Him and come alongside what He is up to when we "set the stage." We can create spiritual space, or an environment, in which God's Spirit can move freely. In my book *Spiritual Parenting*, I discuss at length ten environments and how we can create them as places to put God on display in our children's lives, giving our kids a chance to flex those faith muscles in the process. (The environments are listed in appendix A.)

Live In, Not More Of

There's nothing magical about these ten environments, but they help give language and culture to a church that desires to allow God's Spirit to move and teach. These environments are not things we are encouraging children to be *more of.* For example, we are not asking kids to be more loving, more respectful, or better servants. Rather, we want to create environments where kids see love and respect modeled, or where they have opportunities to serve and be served. They get to *live in* a context where these things are evident, where they get to see God's Spirit at work in and through them. Kids benefit from the opportunities provided or the spillover of the adults who are living in the Spirit. See the difference?

One way to look at this concept is to think of an environment as a climate. We often think of our family of origin as setting the climate in our homes. What was the climate of your home while you were growing up? Was it hostile and self-protective, or was it loving and grace-filled? Either of those, or any combination, shaped who you are today. That environment of your home led you to see the world around you through a specific lens either for good or for bad. The same can be true in our ministries—the climate or environment we set will or will not allow the children in them to be shaped by the things that are true of God and His kingdom.

Creating these environments becomes *our part* in ministry. While we seek what God is doing specifically in the lives of each child and family in our ministry, environments serve as general places where we have seen God's Spirit move throughout history.

The Temptation: Moral Formation

John Coe said the Christian life is about a certain kind of obedience and effort. It's the opening up of the heart to a relationship. It's participation in the vine. Dependence upon the indwelling Spirit. Abiding in Christ. This is our obedience. This is what the spiritual disciplines are actually all about.

Coe said, "I don't want to be a good boy anymore. I don't want to fix myself. I can't fix myself. I want to learn to give up on the project and open more deeply to Christ's work and the work of the Spirit in my deep. But I am still daily tempted by moral formation."[2]

The apostle Paul knew we would be tempted by this. He said,

> O foolish Galatians! Who has bewitched you? It
> was before your eyes that Jesus Christ was publicly
> portrayed as crucified. Let me ask you only this:
> Did you receive the Spirit by works of the law or
> by hearing with faith? Are you so foolish? Having
> begun by the Spirit, are you now being perfected by
> the flesh? (Gal. 3:1–3 ESV)

Think of how ironic this is. Who on earth would be tempted to be moral? We commonly think of ourselves tempted to be immoral, but Paul understood that the life of the Christian would include both. We in fact find ourselves in the temptation of moral formation. We have this little guilt meter inside us, put there by our loving parents, the church, and our sinful human nature. It beckons us to want to make ourselves better.

We have the opportunity to allow a new generation to think differently—to think, *Yes, I'm sinful, yes, I'm broken, but* I can't *fix myself. Only the Holy Spirit can.* This will require our children to have an intimate relationship with Him, to know Him, to hear His voice, to depend upon Him, and not to get up tomorrow to simply *try harder*.

We need to be diligent, because the temptation is so implicit in our curricula and in the way that we speak. We often give take-home assignments for application that essentially say, "Go home this week and just … *be better*. Try to be kinder to your brother, serve more around the house, and be more patient." All these things are good, but they're just *not enough*. And my fear is that we're ultimately sending the wrong message. This message will be abandoned because it simply doesn't work.

Jake's Story

Jake has abandoned church—worse, he has abandoned his faith in Christ. Once a leader in children's ministry and on the worship team in his youth group, he has decided to "experience" God through nature, world religions, and a myriad of drugs. "It didn't work for me," he says. "It's all good, but it just doesn't work that way. You don't just say 'yes' to Jesus and then 'poof' you're all sanctified and holy. That's what people said would happen, but it didn't. My life was and is so full of what you call 'sin,' and I tried walking with God. So where was He? Why didn't He clean up my sin?"

If you aren't bothered by these words, I'm not sure what words would do it. These are the worst possible ones we could hear from a "product" of our ministries to children! It is time to take serious responsibility for the way we communicate the gospel, a relationship with God through Christ, and a life of dependence on God's Spirit.

There are so many things we want to correct in Jake's perspective, but if we were to look objectively at the content and methods in our ministries, do they not often lead to this way of thinking? As kids are connecting the dots of what we are teaching, are those dots leading them to join in on what God is up to or leading them to a life of trying harder in their own power? Because one option is freedom while the other is failure.

The Wind and Sail

Several years ago, my husband and I had the privilege of owning a sailboat. For my husband it was the fulfillment of a lifelong dream after decades of sailing. For me, it was my very first experience on the sea with a sail. I remember the first time he took me out. In anticipation, I prepared myself for an epic day on the ocean, the adventure of racing out to the horizon. However, when our boat left the safety of the harbor and hit the open waters … *nothing happened*. We simply sat there, bobbing up and down without even a balmy breeze to call our own. I shouted to my husband to make the boat go faster, but he just laughed. He said, "There's no wind today."

Not long after that day, we went out again. This time I was skeptical about the adventure part and focused on preparing delicacies in the hull of the ship. Yet this day was different. As our boat sailed past the safety of the harbor, we slammed into wind and waves like I had never seen. My husband scrambled to get our sails into position, and off we went like a race car into the open waters. The boat was heeling to one side while chips and salsa flew through the air. I shouted to my husband to make the boat slow down, but he just laughed. He said, "I can't—the wind is in charge today."

As ministers of Christ, I believe our job is to simply hoist up our sail as far and as wide as we can and catch the wind of God. That sail is important, but not nearly as important as the wind. When we allow God's Spirit to be captain and we submit to Him to charter the course ahead, we get a sense of what it means to depend on Him and wait for God's Spirit to *blow*. Of course we can choose to take down our sails at any point and motor in our own direction at our own pace, but that is not the life we are called to. That is not the life that will be compelling for this generation, either. Once you're awakened to the wind, nothing else will satisfy.

Ministry Sails

What are the sails in our ministries? These things allow the Spirit to move powerfully in our midst, but we need to keep in mind that they are merely there for His use, when and as He chooses. Some ministry sails may include programs, positions, room décor, themes, curriculum, and other structures. When we look at the role the Spirit may want to assume in our ministries, how can we begin to assess each of these in light of His presence?

One such assessment led us to remove our Bible Buck Store and place a prayer wall, cross, and giving box as worship centers for parents and kids to visit before and after the service. As you can imagine, I wasn't very popular the day we took out all the cool toys and replaced them with a dimly lit worship station. But I wanted to proclaim that this time to be with God was sacred or different from what the world had to offer, and over time the kids and parents began to crave it and be changed by it!

Right as you walked into our children's ministry area, there was now a place where you could give offerings together. If you were a parent and you wanted to drop off your offering check, you could, and if you were a seven-year-old, you could put in your quarters. Together you could worship as a family. There was also a cross and an area to write prayers on a wall. Often we witnessed families praying together as they dropped off their children for church.

Families Learning Together

One day, right before the service started, a young single mom came in with her son and told me it was her first time there. She said, "In fact it's my first time to church since I was a little girl." She went on to say, "I'm not good at this; I don't know what to do." Instead of inviting her to step right up to my Bible Buck Store, I was able to lead her to the cross and prayer wall. I said, "You can pray with your son here, and I'll show you how." I asked if there was something that I could pray for them about, and she told me, so I prayed with them for that. I watched as she held her son's hand in hers and they sat there praying together. I wondered if this was the first time this family had ever done this. I was so blessed by it, and I could tell they were blessed too.

She left and went to church, and her son stayed in our ministry. Later when we had our own worship time and the kids were singing, we invited the students to go to any of the worship centers that they wanted to. I watched as that little boy got up, went straight to the cross that he had prayed at with his mom, and began to pray. When his mom showed up after service, he took her to the cross and said with excitement, "Mom, during church I prayed again here just like you showed me, and I know God heard me." As she left, she said to me, "You know, I've heard about Jesus my entire life, but today was the first day that I *experienced* Him. Thank you."

This was all I needed to propel me to look at other things in my ministry through the lens of "What environment am I really creating?" In this example, a Bible Buck Store wasn't bad, but it didn't facilitate the environment that I wanted to create where children and their parents could experience God's Spirit. In chapter 9 we will go into more depth about ways we can create an environment for children to respond to God's voice or promptings in the context of a worship service.

Dreaming of More

Once we tasted how God could change our lives and the lives of those in our ministry by shifting the way that we approached our current paradigm, nothing was off limits. We began to *dream of more*! In fact, together we penned these words to encourage ourselves not to give up or lose hope in the "in-between time"—the time between our envisioned future and our present reality:

> **Imagine a Generation**
> - Children/students worship from the inside out, compelled by the Spirit—not through behaving in expected or mandated ways, but through seeing worship as a lifestyle instead of as a moment or event.
> - Children/students possess a kingdom community mind-set and choose to usher in the realities of justice, mercy, love, the presence of God, forgiveness, humility, and service to life in everyday situations.
> - Children/students live with a global awareness, feel responsible for their brothers and sisters around the world, and feel compelled to make Christ known to every corner of the globe within their lifetime.

- Children/students are knowledgeable about God's Word, but even better, through it have come to know God personally. They have investigated the Scriptures for themselves and have concluded that God's Word is Truth and are unashamed of it.
- Children/students know God's voice, desire to obey it, and then obey it in and through the power of the Holy Spirit as they depend on Him alone for strength.

Each of these statements became our marching orders. We prayerfully sought how God wanted us to respond to Him to create environments where we gave prime real estate to making worship a lifestyle and not just the singing portion of our service. We considered in what practical ways we could allow the kids in our ministry to feel that they were a part of God's kingdom here and now every time they put into practice the markers of His coming kingdom, or even how they were attached to their brothers and sisters around the world in a global big-C Church. We evaluated in what ways we provided opportunities for our kids to flex their faith muscles with those who didn't yet know Jesus and to sense both the calling and responsibility on their lives to be His ambassadors to those people.

Investigating the Bible

Every corner in our ministry plans was searched. Nothing was safe. And just when we thought we were done with our transformation, we then sensed God asking us to look deeper: into our curriculum, the way we taught and represented God's Word, along with how and when we allowed the children to investigate it for themselves.

Most of our kids were not bringing their Bibles, and it simply became easier to project the Bible passages onto the large screens in the room. There is nothing wrong with this, and it can be quite helpful for many kids. But we wanted kids to actually hold Bibles in their hands, shuffle through the pages, become familiar with the layout, and have the satisfaction of finding the passage for themselves. Further, we wanted them to perhaps read it with fresh eyes of discovery, to see what came before in the context and what came after. We began to take the necessary steps to make sure every child had a Bible as well as to carve out time to pass them out.

Time to Listen

Of course we wanted the kids in our ministry to hear God's voice, but we had to ask the deafening question of whether we had allocated time and space for them to do just that. When you are programming a service, every minute is precious! Would we give prime real estate for "listening" when so many other things demanded those minutes? We had to. If we believed the things we were saying, we *had* to. And so it began. After our time in God's Word, there was a time to sit quietly and listen and then to respond (more about this in chapter 9). Those were humble days, filled with excitement and even some regret.

I can tell you that our assessment was not what I had expected. Before this time, I believed that my ministry was solid, teaching and proclaiming God in every way. By the time I was done,

however, there was *nothing* that had not been modified in some
way to create an environment to put God's Spirit in His proper
place—and to do so more intentionally, with a grid to assess our
ministry efforts.

MINISTRY ASSESSMENT

Take time to reflect, respond, and dream about how God might use
the concept of hearing from God in your life personally or in your
ministry to children and their families.

Reflect

After reading about the Holy Spirit's role both in transformation
and empowerment, where do you feel you may have neglected to
put up a sail to catch His wind? In what ways have you perhaps
motored your way in your own direction or at your own speed in
your personal spiritual life? In your ministry? In what ways has
God's Spirit convicted you as you have been awakened to His
purposes? Where in your life have you allowed the temptation
of moral formation to quench what God's Spirit might be up
to? Spend some time writing an account of your thoughts and
reflections.

Respond

Take some time to respond to God based on the things He has
revealed to you. Is this a time of repentance or humility? Is this a time
to seek wisdom and guidance? Is this a time for creative anticipation
and ideating? However God's Spirit is speaking to you right now,
respond to Him in that with petition and thanksgiving.

Dream

Next, what dreams has God inspired in you for the children and families in your ministry? If you were to write your own dream statements of an envisioned generation, what statements would come to mind? How might the things He has revealed to you be catalysts to assess each area in your ministry to children and their families? Where can your story be shared or translated into a ministry opportunity?

6

HEAR IT AND DO IT

Flexing Those Faith Muscles

We are saved by faith alone, but the
faith that saves is never alone.
Philip Melanchthon, from a letter to Martin Luther

I recently had a conversation with a twentysomething who was raised in the church ministry that I oversaw years ago. Today I would characterize her faith as apathetic. She isn't exactly renouncing her faith, but she isn't living it either. What factors led her to this place, I wondered? Had she not experienced God? His power? Had she not heard the truth? Did she not have a chance to put her faith into action? And what about her parents? Did we lead them in ways that would equip them to lead her?

These unanswered questions have convinced me that leading families has become one of the greatest challenges of our time. This is a complex generation, facing incredible uncertainty and darkness, at risk of abandoning faith altogether. How can we be used by God to respond effectively and help families grow strong faith muscles?

Faith Muscles Grow When They Are Used

First, I believe faith muscles get flabby when they're not used, but they grow strong when they are flexed. Our families are suffering from lethargy of faith because of atrophied muscles. For most Christians in the Western world today, our relatively comfortable way of life has eradicated our need to walk by faith and depend on God. This loss of dependence has caused weak or absent faith. Yet "without faith it is impossible to please God" (Heb. 11:6). So how do we create an environment where children and their parents can actually flex their faith muscles until they're strong?

The book of James reminds us that our life of genuine faith is one that is put into action. The children in our ministries can be inspired by this truth from an intellectual perspective, but we must give them the opportunity to act on it. Faith is a muscle that must be used!

Creating Space for Children to Respond

Several years ago I was leading a group of elementary students through the book of James. At the conclusion of our eight-week study together, I was compelled by this idea of wanting them to flex their faith muscles. I didn't plan a new study right away. I wanted to take our next time together to explore what could be next. The kids arrived and sat down as usual to hear the next Bible study, but this time there was none.

Instead I asked them, "Children, how can *you* put your faith into action? You've heard these things from God's Word for the past eight weeks. You've learned that God wants us to not just be 'hearers' of His Word, but 'doers' also. So, what are you going to *do* about what you've *heard*?"

At first there was silence. The kids just stared back at me. I realized that I had never asked them such a thing. This wasn't what they were expecting. They didn't know how to answer. So I kept pressing, asking them to ask God how they might respond to what they had heard.

I confess there was a part of me that desperately wanted to validate my teaching and give them suggestions for action steps that they could simply agree with. I didn't want to consider that with all we had done to truly investigate Scripture, it had fallen exclusively into the abyss of biblical information stored securely away in the archives of a child's brain. No! I wanted to see *life transformation*. If I'm honest, I wanted to know that God was still in the business of raising up individuals whose faith "the world was not worthy of" (Heb. 11:38).

I didn't give in. At this point, my faith was hanging in the balance as much as theirs was. "What are you going to do now that you have heard the words of God and how He wants us to live?" It felt like an eternity in waiting. I was uncomfortable. My leaders were uncomfortable. The kids were … well, bored.

But then one courageous hand rose in the back. The young girl said, "We could help the homeless people." My heart leapt! "Yes, we could do that! What else could we do to put our faith into action?" I asked. Soon more children began to chime in with ideas that ranged from eliminating global hunger to knitting sweaters for cold dogs.

An Idea Fleshed Out

After some hearty brainstorming, we finally landed on an idea that was actually doable. There was a local motel ministry with which our church was in relationship. Living there were families who had been displaced from their homes or were in some kind of transition, some fleeing from abuse. The thought that we could pack sack lunches for the families who lived there so that the children would have a healthy meal at school was what seemed to ignite faith in our group.

In order for them to further flex their faith muscles, we asked the kids to come up with how we would mobilize this, how we would gather the lunch supplies, and even what items would go into the lunch. Of course it would have been easier to give the idea to a group of moms and have them work out the details, but the kids were the ones who were supposed to be flexing their faith muscles.

I was encouraged to see that with a little guidance they were all working together and making great decisions about what should go into the lunch bags. Then one child said, "We can't forget the note." Ah, the note. This one child stated that his favorite part of the lunch was the note from his mom. So we started thinking about how this note could be a note *from God*.

The day finally arrived for us to assemble the lunches. Stations were set up all over the room to decorate the lunch bags, to make the sandwiches, to fill the bag with chips or a piece of fruit. But there was one station that allowed the kids to write the "notes from God." I printed out note cards that said, "Dear one" on the top, then left a blank area (for the child to write a note), and then closed it with, "Love, God." At first I felt the need to help them. After all, writing on behalf of God was serious business. I didn't want them to get it wrong. I took out a white board and began to write suggested things God might say to a person in such a situation.

No sooner had my hand begun to write on the white board than I felt convicted. God's Spirit was urging me, "Don't you believe that I can speak to these children? Don't you want Me to be the One who speaks? Don't you want these children to use faith to listen to Me?" I realized that this was how this whole thing began in the first place. I had a desire for these kids to flex their faith muscles, and yet here I was offering to lift this "weight" for them.

I quickly erased my trite words from the board and urged the children to pray and ask *God* what they should write. I began to tell them that *God* knew who was going to get their note in their lunch. I told them that there was something *He* wanted to say to that person, and He could use their faith to accomplish this. I watched those kids praying like I had never seen them pray before. One girl would pray, then write, then pray again, then write. It was as if she was penning actual words from God. We packed over four hundred lunches that night, and we tucked a little note in each one. In faith, we waited.

A Love Note from God

The next day, our representative to the motel went from door to door, passing out the lunches to each child. He came to a room where a mom cautiously opened the door and peeked out. She accepted the two lunches for her children but also humbly asked if she could take one for herself. So he handed her the three lunches and closed the door.

What nobody knew was that early that morning, this mom had woken up in total desperation. She had just been through an ugly divorce. She had been physically abused; she had lost her home and her job. She had nothing. She was now living in this motel with her two kids, and life had lost all hope. As the reality of the day set in, she began to cry out to God, lamenting, "You've forgotten me, YOU'VE FORGOTTEN ME!" In this moment of hopelessness, she decided that she was going to end her life. She had arranged for her children to go to school and to be picked up by her sister, and in the meantime she would kill herself in order to stop the suffering.

As her two children left for school as planned, she saw her lunch bag that was sitting on the counter. It had a cross on it. One of the children had decorated the outside of the bag with a beautiful cross beside a colorful rainbow. This woman remembered being a little girl who went to church, hearing about Jesus, but she had long since felt forgotten, used, and abused. Yet something in her reached out and grabbed that lunch. As she looked inside, the very first thing she pulled out was the little note. With trembling hands, she opened it to read these words: "Dear one, I have *not forgotten you*. Love, God."

Faith Inextinguishable

It's almost unbelievable, isn't it? God spoke to a child to write those words. Then God made sure *that note* got placed in *that lunch* for *that mom* on *that day*. Who is this God that we serve? He is a God who never forgets and always redeems! His story is one of redemption, and we have the opportunity to play a part in it. The faith stories of the kids in our ministry are not ones of us simply telling them *what* to do; rather it's giving them the *opportunity to do it*.

The testimony of this woman's life and her experience that day revolutionized the kids' faith in my ministry. They were radically changed. Their faith had been tested and put into action, and now they would never see their mission in life the same. Quite simply, they were unstoppable. Before their years of middle school were completed, they had started more ministry opportunities in our community than could be counted. They walked dogs for the elderly, knitted blankets for the homeless in the inner city, bought Bibles for schoolmates, sent care packages to those in the armed services, and sang to shut-ins in the retirement homes, just to name a few things. The world was not worthy of them.

Faith Is Rooted in Truth

Certainly, not every time we ask our kids to flex those faith muscles will something so miraculous be apparent. Perhaps we will see the fruit, and perhaps we won't. But this is the God we serve. He is capable of such life transformation. Whether we see it or not is secondary. Our faith comes into play again as we continue to put it into practice regardless of the outcome our eyes can see. We live it out … by faith.

As our kids enter adolescence, they need to understand another question: "What does it mean to live for my faith?" This young generation is hungry to know that this faith we embrace really matters. In order for them to navigate the oppression of the world and the tactics of the Enemy, they will need to *know truth*.

This new generation is eclectic with cut-and-paste values and nonlinear thinking. They are different from any other generation, and yet it is estimated that they will outnumber any other generation that has lived in North American history. However, we know the statistics that these young people are walking away from their faith and into darkness at an alarming rate. This tells me that they have missed the truth. People don't walk away *from the truth*; they walk away *in search of truth*. When you know the truth—really know it—it transforms you! When you *don't* have the truth, it's as the Bible says—"people loved the darkness rather than the light because their works were evil" (John 3:19 ESV).

Furthermore Romans 1:25 says that ungodliness and depravity are a result of exchanging the truth of God for a lie. We do this when we allow society to substitute truth with alternatives or relativity. Many teenagers today will argue that truth is always relative to the individual and the circumstance. While many of these will also describe themselves as followers of Christ and say that the Bible is accurate in all of its teachings, they nevertheless believe that truth is more accurately based on individual feelings and experiences.

A Truth Worth Dying For

We need to deal with this misunderstanding of truth in our ministries. Jesus alone said, "I am … the truth…. No one comes to the Father except through me" (John 14:6) and further, the truth that He offers will set you free (John 8:32). I often think of Stephen, the first recorded martyr in the Bible. I've always been struck by this young man's understanding of truth. A truth that he had no question about dying for. I can guarantee you that this man had the truth instilled so deeply within that *living his faith* was merely an overflow.

> Now Stephen, a man full of God's grace and power,
> performed great wonders and signs among the peo-
> ple. Opposition arose, however, from members of the
> Synagogue of the Freedmen (as it was called)—Jews
> of Cyrene and Alexandria as well as the provinces of
> Cilicia and Asia—who began to argue with Stephen.
> But they could not stand up against the wisdom the
> Spirit gave him as he spoke. (Acts 6:8–10)

Later, in Acts 7:59–60 we read that before he died, Stephen even prayed for God not to hold the sins of those who killed him against them. Ultimately, truth transforms the way we live. What does it mean to live for our faith? It means to be *transformed* by the undeniable truth of who Jesus claims to be.

A Chance to Live by Truth

I attended a Christian school during high school, and during my junior year I was privileged to have a Bible teacher who desired to take us from merely memorizing the content of our faith to actually putting reality into our understanding of what it means to live as Christians. We were studying the first-century Christians and the persecution they faced. He started a semester-long game entitled "The Underground." I will never forget this experience.

Our teacher secretly identified each person in our class as a believer, a nonbeliever, or a Roman authority. The believers were all given colored paper clips as a sign of their faith. Contrary to my hopes, I was assigned the role of a "Christian," a part of "the Way." After all, I had been a Christian my entire life, and for me, at the ripe age of seventeen, it was already becoming a bit mundane. I was hoping for some action, and all I got was the "same ole, same ole"—at least that was what I thought at the time.

The game started with the Christians receiving instructions about the underground church on returned homework assignments. At lunch we met together in secret places on campus. There we read Scripture, worshipped, were warned against the authorities and the plots of the Evil One. Our teacher encouraged us to be strong and to make every effort to courageously spread the good news through the power of God's Spirit. We were commissioned to grow the underground church by sharing the good news of our own life transformation.

For weeks I was fearful to say anything about my faith, watching how people were acting, trying to find out who the players were. When a believer led a nonbeliever to grace, they were given a paper clip and invited to the underground church service. Several times we had to change the location of the church in order not to be caught by the authorities.

One day, when I shared the good news with a friend and invited her to the underground, she smiled sweetly and then pulled out from her pocket a chain of ten paper clips. I knew immediately what that meant. The clips represented the martyrs whose deaths she was responsible for. I knew that I would be next. "Bring me to your church, or you will die," she said. "Deny your Christ, or I will have your life!" *This is only a game*, I kept telling myself as I was thrown before the judge and sentenced to die.

The following day I was tied up in ropes and escorted to the courtyard, where students gathered for lunch. I was among four Christians walking to their deaths that day. One of the other teachers began to speak: "Fellow citizens, we have here those who have broken the law and have rebelled against Rome, the domain of Caesar, by proclaiming another king: Jesus. For this, they must die. The Jewish law calls for them to be stoned. Citizens, I give to you these four lawbreakers. Do with them as you wish."

With that, the entire student body began shouting and throwing stones (albeit paper ones) at us. As we were hit, we fell to the ground. Clutching together, overwhelmed with the reality of this moment, one student whispered to me, "Michelle, today you will be with Jesus in paradise." I began to cry. This was no longer a game. This was real. I thought of Stephen, the first martyr. What was it about his faith that allowed him to do this—for real, with such faith and courage?

For weeks, I spent my lunch hour in my Bible teacher's room, debriefing and learning about people who were being martyred all over the world every day—today! Finally, after many discussions and tears, my teacher recognized my consumption with martyrdom and said something to me that I will never forget. He said, "Michelle, God may *never ask you* to die for your faith, but I can guarantee that He *will ask you*, every day, to *live* for it!"

That was a pivotal moment in my Christian faith. This idea of being willing to die for my faith compelled me to know what was truth and what was not, but the idea of living for my faith also compelled me toward that same truth and stretched my faith in even deeper ways.

Faith Demonstrated in Obedience

We have accounts in the Gospels where Jesus experienced others' faith, and when He did, He was *amazed*. He stopped and applauded it every time He witnessed it in action. Jesus was amazed when He encountered a Roman centurion's faith on display: "I have not found anyone in Israel with such great faith" (Matt. 8:10). He acknowledged it, responded to it, and blessed it. Likewise, when Jesus expected to see it and didn't, He would chastise, "O, you of little faith!" Faith is a really big deal to our God. And He's given us the commission to pass it on to our children.

Conviction, Surrender, Behavior

I shared earlier about some of my experience teaching a group of elementary students. In that class, it was simple to learn with our minds the biblical definition of faith: a firm conviction and personal surrender that manifest in *corresponding behavior*. James wrote,

> Show me your faith without deeds, and I will show you my faith by my deeds. You believe that there is one God. Good! Even the demons believe that— and shudder.
>
> You foolish person, do you want evidence that faith without deeds is useless? … As the body without the spirit is dead, so faith without deeds is dead. (2:18–20, 26)

James cautioned against adopting a solely intellectual belief system of biblical knowledge and the things that we *say* we believe.

More Than Just Doing Good Stuff

At the same time, however, there are other places in Scripture where we see Jesus condemning people for simply *doing things* in the flesh but not actually being led by the Spirit or by His power to do those things. It's not about just "doing good stuff."

I've had to stop on many occasions and assess my ministry to children. In what ways might I have communicated that the Christian life was about "doing good stuff"—and of course, "not doing the bad stuff"? Perhaps I did it in ignorance or because it seemed simpler to communicate the *end result*. Because in the end, the good stuff will be there. It's there not because I did it, but because as I walk in faith, God produces that in me.

The ministry to the family in this generation must straddle the age-old tension between faith and works. James's compelling argument is that we can't have one without the other. I agree. The challenge comes in *how* we ignite this kind of ministry within our churches. How can we engage families in a growing, vibrant faith based on truth *and* the overflow action of that faith? Jesus reminds us that obedience will be the foundation of this journey.

More Than Good Knowledge

In Matthew 7:24–27, Jesus said that everyone who *hears these words* and *puts them into practice* is like a wise man who built his house on the rock. The foundations refer to how someone hears the truth and then either chooses to put the truth into practice—obey—or chooses not to put it into practice and disobey.

This is the faith and action partnership. It's putting into practice what we believe. It's not simply hearing God's Word—because the foolish man heard it and didn't put it into practice. When we think about ministry to kids and their parents from a perspective of passing on our faith to the next generation, then building on rock means obeying God's Word in our everyday circumstances and letting kids be not only eyewitnesses to that rock-solid way of living but participants in it too. This becomes faith that is worth *living* and *dying* for.

One of the greatest challenges in family ministry today is to help families ask the questions, *How would I order all of my life based on faith? Erasing the line between the sacred and the secular? Bringing all that I am to a place of living sacrifice? What wouldn't that include? How would Jesus live my life if He were me?* These are the thought processes of a faith disciple and the narrative that actually precedes the story of the two foundations.

In Matthew 7:13–23, Jesus sets the parameters for those entering into a faith relationship. The gate is narrow, and few will find it, He cautions. False prophets will try to water it down or sabotage it. People of true faith will bear fruit, and it will be good fruit. It will be fruit consistent with the tree. In other words, one's words and actions will be congruent. Not everyone who says, "Lord, Lord" in that day will be saved.

These are some very sobering words of Jesus that inform the story of the two foundations of which our children so gleefully sing. I wonder sometimes, by the way I have led children's and family ministry, if I am actually getting what He is saying.

James told us that our faith will be tested. This testing will bring endurance and will move us to rely upon Christ's wisdom and strength. When children and their parents see this testing as an opportunity to flex their faith muscles, then they begin to understand what it means to live by faith.

Creating Space for Families to Practice What They Know

Families are busier than ever. Faith in action from a heart of obedience will take time. As we shepherd children, we may need to consider eliminating a good program in order to create an opportunity that might be better. An opportunity that gives them a chance to "hear it and do it." In one ministry I led, I began family experiences that helped parents and kids respond to the Bible study series that we had just finished. I gave up our quarterly family movie nights in order to create space to do this. Not everyone saw this as the better choice, but I knew this was what God was asking from me.

Another ministry held three "Hear It and Do It" weekends throughout the year that allowed the entire church to participate in this idea of faith in action. Annual mission trips were also tangible ways we were able to *put into practice* the abundance of things that the community had learned throughout the year. Consider in what areas God might be asking you to take a step of obedience.

Faith Flows from Relationship with God

Obedient faith comes from knowing God and hearing His voice. When we have these, we have a relationship with Him from which a *desire* to obey flows. This obedience is then *empowered* through God's Spirit, not through our own fortitude of trying harder. We take little steps each day to enter deeper and deeper into a relationship with God and to align our will and actions with His. This is obedient faith.

Without this life-giving relationship, all we have is good knowledge and outward conformity, a husk without the nourishing grain. Such counterfeit faith sends young adults walking away in search of some other "truth" that seems to work.

As leaders, then, we need to put our faith into practice by considering the focus of our ministries. It has always been God's plan to have one generation be the bearer of the message to the next generation. In many ways we have failed to do this effectively. It's time for us to wake up to faith and reclaim the territory in our churches and in our homes to allow this generation to put their faith into action and to intentionally create those environments that encourage them to put flesh on faith.

How can we start today? Consider these five key ideas discussed in this chapter:

- Faith muscles grow when they are used.
- Faith is rooted in truth that matters.
- Faith demonstrates itself in obedience.
- Faith flows from relationship with God.
- Faith is passed on from generation to generation.

MINISTRY ASSESSMENT

Take time to reflect, respond, and dream about how God might use these five truths about faith in your life personally or in your ministry to children and their families.

Reflect

After reading about God's design for faith in action, how have you practically been able to flex your faith muscles this past month? Ministry season? In what ways has God's Spirit convicted you about living out a life of faith? Where in your life have you allowed your faith muscles to atrophy? What things have led to these weak faith muscles? Or where have you been flexing them with strong results? Spend some time writing an account of your thoughts and reflections.

Respond

Take some time to respond to God based on what He has revealed to you. Is this a time of confession or celebration? Is this a time to repent? Is this a time for quietness and solitude? Or is this a time of rejoicing and thanksgiving? However God's Spirit is speaking to you right now, respond to Him in that with a heart of surrender.

Dream

What dreams has God inspired in you for cultivating environments for children and their families to put faith into action? Is there a specific story that has come to mind where God has shown this kind of faith to you? Is there a particular next step that you can begin implementing immediately? How might the things He has revealed to you be catalysts to make some adjustments in your ministry to children and their families? As you look at the five key ideas of faith above, which one is most in need of correction or modification in your ministry today?

7

FINDING YOUR PLACE IN THE BIG GOD STORY

A Story of Redemption

To better understand [the Bible], we will need to view it with a dual lens. [The] individual stories from the Bible [are] our Lower Story. The Lower Story reveals the here and now of daily life, the experiences and circumstances we see here on earth.... But [God] has a higher agenda than our survival and comfort.... The Bible isn't filled with a thousand individual stories of God's intervention just to get people through rough times,

but rather one grand story of something larger,
something eternal. This is the Upper Story.

Randy Frazee, The Heart of the Story

I remember being compelled as a young adult by the metanarrative of Scripture. After being raised in a Christian home and a Bible-teaching church, I finally had the ultimate "aha" moment when I discovered that the Bible was not just a collection of Sunday school stories about the good guys and the bad guys, but rather a continuous epic storyline of a loving God redeeming all of creation back into right relationship with Himself.

One story. One main character. One God loving me.

It's Really True

And it's a true story! There's a small church in southern California that meets in a nightclub and holds children's church in the green room. This unique church venue reflects the passion of the pastor to reach people who wouldn't normally come to a traditional service. The church service is mostly filled with brand-new Christians. And because the parents are brand-new Christians, the kids are brand-new Christians, and the Big God Story is completely new to them.

In the green room of the nightclub, my friend Debbie had been telling the Big God Story from the beginning—relating to the kids how God promised to send the Redeemer who would restore our relationship with God. Over many months, she unfolded for them how the promised Redeemer—Jesus—was eventually born as a baby, lived a sinless life, and then died for our sins.

One day, when it was pouring rain outside, a little girl sat listening as my friend told the part of the Big God Story when Jesus was born in Bethlehem. The girl's eyes grew bigger and bigger as she listened. Then the girl interrupted, asking, "Is this true?"

"Yes!" my friend enthusiastically replied. The little girl's jaw dropped open wide enough to reveal her tiny molars. As my friend continued to read, the little girl sat there with her mouth hanging open in shock. Then she interrupted again—"Is this *really* true? Are you sure?"

"Yes!" my friend replied. "It's *really* true."[1]

Because we've heard the story so many times, we might be tempted to gloss over the amazement that it's all really true. God really did promise to send the Redeemer, He really kept the promise alive throughout history, He really sent His Son to die for us, and He really redeemed us from our sin because He really loves us that much! The Big God Story is amazing—and true! And sometimes it takes a new believer—a child—to remind us how shocking it truly is.

Information and Transformation

After participating for many years in ministry to children and youth, I was surprised that we continued to teach isolated Bible "stories" with little or no context to the whole. I became concerned to see literacy of *biblical information* within what Randy Frazee calls "the Lower Story," stories of individual people in the Bible such as Noah, David, or Paul—yet without *transformation* from "the Upper Story" of redemption and relationship.

So that's when I decided to do something crazy. I wanted to try to teach God's Word as *one* storyline and to teach it chronologically as well. Of course this would present some apparent problems. If we began teaching creation (Genesis) in the fall quarter, we wouldn't be able to get through the entire Old Testament before December, when Jesus was to be born at Christmas (in the church calendar). On top of this, we wouldn't be able to align Easter (and its ever-changing dates) on schedule with His death and resurrection and still have enough of the New Testament to take us through the remainder of spring and all of summer. As practitioners, we have always lived in the world of "scope and sequence" and church holidays, right? This idea just seemed absurd.

Yet after considering the multitude of problems that might arise from teaching the Bible as a chronological narrative, I decided to take the plunge anyway. I wondered if what we would *gain* from telling God's Story as it was intended would prove of more value than our *inconveniences*.

One of our solutions was to tell about the birth of Christ in the winter through the perspective of Old Testament prophecy, and we could pause on Easter to simply tell the entire Big God Story with an emphasis on His death and resurrection. After only nine months into our pilot study of this methodology, one elementary boy became impatient—in a good way.

You see, when you teach the Bible as one story and not a collection of stories, there is a natural cliff-hanger moment every week. It's a continuing storyline, and the idea of coming back next week to hear what *happens next* is naturally woven into the text.

One week, this young man went home on a mission. He couldn't take the suspense any longer. He took out his young reader's Bible (a condensed version of the actual text) and read it from start to finish.

Then, when Sunday arrived, he burst through the classroom doors and garnered everyone's attention. "All right everyone," he shouted, "I went home, I read the whole thing … and we're all going to be okay … Jesus is coming back!"

In over twenty years of ministry to children at that point, I had never heard of a child motivated to read the whole thing in one week because he was so captivated by the story! I realized that in the past I had inadvertently made the story so small. Paul and Silas got out of jail, Daniel was not eaten by the ravenous lions, and Ruth and Boaz lived happily ever after. There was no need to find out what happens *next*.

What Story Are Your Children Living?

We are designed to love stories and to live stories. We all live inside a story, whether we recognize it or not. We tell ourselves a story of what the world is about, what's important, and what our place in the story is. Yet our culture bombards our children with a story that says that life is "all about me." It tells them that they are born by chance, that life is about getting what they want and being happy, and that death is the end of the story.

The Bible tells a different story, an epic story of the Father pursuing His children in order to have a personal relationship with each one of them. This story is "all about God." It tells children that they are born because God wants them and made them in His image, that life is about knowing and loving Him, and that death is not at all the end of the story. It tells them that the Big God Story, which began long ago, has been lived by people for many centuries, is going somewhere exciting, has a place for each one of us, and is centered on Jesus, our Messiah.

As children, our world is very small. We see *everything* from our vantage point and how it affects us directly or indirectly. It's only as we mature (hopefully) that we begin to see the world as much more complex, and we begin to see our role as servants addressing the needs of those around us.

Dangerous Lie

Sometimes I am tempted to believe that *I* am the main character, that the story is really about me—because after all, I am in every scene. But that's a lie. It's a lie that the children in our world today are told on every TV channel, in every advertisement, and in every song. Sometimes it's blatant and sometimes subtle, but nonetheless children are being made to believe that the greatest story ever told is happening in their obscure little world.

Can you see how dangerous Satan's lie is? If he can get me to believe that this life is a story centered around me and my happiness, then I will see life as a series of events that allow me either to succeed or fail in this endeavor. I begin to manipulate people and events to my own benefit. After all, don't we always want the main character to be victorious in the end? We want her to succeed and be happy. Thus, my happiness becomes primary. The problem with this perspective is that life is sometimes hard and unfair. I can't always control life, events, and other people. Then what? And even when I do manage to control people, that's not what I or they were created for. In using them to make my life work, I harm them.

If we consistently tell our children the Big God Story and help them to see the bigger story that has been lived out for thousands of years, they will have the privilege of catching a glimpse of the wonder of it all. The wonderful mystery of who God is and how He has chosen a part for each of us to play. We can never play the role of the main character, but when we understand why we can't, we rest in the knowledge that we were never created to do so. When this happens, we are able to worship God and not ourselves. We are free to be who we were created to be: true worshippers in every aspect of our lives!

The Connective Tissue

Matthew 1 and Luke 3 recount records of the genealogy of Jesus Christ. If you read the records, they reveal the men and women that Jesus was related to: Abraham, Isaac, Jacob, Ruth, Jesse, David, Solomon, Ahaz, Hezekiah, Josiah, even Rahab and Tamar—men and women we hear about throughout the Big God Story.

Often, we skip over genealogies. They often mean nothing to us. In fact, they didn't mean anything to me when I read them countless times before. But since I now know the story that God was telling through the lives of these people and the covenants that He made with them, I am astounded. Throughout the Big God Story, God was setting up people, events, and situations to proclaim the promise given to us in the birth, death, and resurrection of Christ—the promised Redeemer.

Throughout the Big God Story we see a thread of love, grace, long-suffering, and holiness from the Author of the story—God Himself. We find startling revelations, seasons of pain or separation, joyful surprises, and answers to long-awaited prayers. We see the ups and downs of relationship. We are impacted by redemption and the immeasurable love of God for each of us.

When reading God's Word as the Big God Story, we begin to discover that this is not a story that merely takes place in the past, but rather one that we are in the very midst of—today. It isn't over! God is using us as He used Moses, Deborah, David, and Mary, offering us a place in His story to further His kingdom until its ultimate fulfillment—when Jesus returns in all His glory and ushers us into an eternal personal relationship free from sin and separation.

We are living and breathing testaments of His redemptive plan. And someday we will look back and praise God for the way our lives played a part in His story. In the same way we have seen God's plan accomplished through the lives of Abraham, Esther, and Joseph, it's thrilling to think that someday we will see how *our* lives have built upon the lives of other believers to further and proclaim the Big God Story.

The Main Character

Let's consider sharing the Bible's content in the context of its original storyline. Often we tell fragmented stories of God, Jesus, or other characters in the Bible, and we do so in ways that aren't linear. Even most children who know the stories of the Bible can't tell you whether Abraham was born before David, or if baby Jesus was alive when baby Moses was.

Stories told in isolation don't tell the bigger story where God is central. Instead, baby Moses is the key figure one day, Noah is the key figure one day, and Jesus is merely the key figure on another occasion. But by putting each story in the context of the main story, we can begin to elevate God, the Redeemer, to His rightful place in the storyline—the main character. We examined this main storyline in my book *Spiritual Parenting*, which tells the story in chronological order, highlighting the promise, preservation, prediction, and presentation of the Christ. Understanding its entirety inspires us to create the Big God Story as a foundational pillar of our teaching ministry.

Impact and Influence

Hearing God's epic story profoundly influenced one student who had been in our ministry for several years. He had heard the Big God Story and learned that he could have a part in that story. The fact that God had him in mind for a role when He wrote the grand narrative inspired him. This thought followed him as he graduated out of our children's ministry and entered into middle school.

Not long after his transition, I received a Facebook request from him. It was entitled, "God has a Big Story, and you can be a part of it." Wow! He had actually heard what we were saying, and he had grasped that God was inviting him into it. The next weekend I asked him what motivated him to create such a group. He said he was amazed that every day at school he could sense that his peers were living their lives aimlessly or without knowledge that something *bigger* was going on around them. He was saddened that they neither knew that God was writing an amazing story nor were aware that they were invited into it by His grace and love.

So his plan seemed simple. He would merely post blog updates after each week at church, recounting what he had learned from the Big God Story, and then ask questions that would provoke others to consider how they might play a part in it. Here was a thirteen-year-old who had been eternally impacted by the *story* in such a profound way that he could not help but live out the gospel.

That's the essence of the Big God Story after all! Good and evil war with each other, evil seems to overtake the world, but then Jesus shows up and brings justice, and we who know Him are saved. He makes everything good, and those who follow Jesus all win in the end! I don't know about you, but I want to be part of *that* story, and I definitely want to be on the winning side. I want to be one of Jesus's friends when He shows up on the scene, and I want Satan to be punished! This is a story kids can relate to, and yet so often we only allow them to see pieces of it at any given time. When we do that, we prevent them from seeing the power of living it and sharing it.

The Gospel

The word *gospel* in the New Testament can be translated "good news." The original Greek word is *euaggelion*. By definition, this word proclaims the good news of the coming Messiah, but it also refers to the Giver of the Messiah, the plans leading up to His coming, and the condition for which the Messiah was needed in the first place. The good news is the *entire* story!

I have erroneously compartmentalized the gospel to exclusively mean the part where Jesus pays the price for my sin. Jesus commissioned us to spread the good news, but if we misunderstand the message as an isolated event, then we will be story bearers of that alone. But if we understand the charge to spread the entire storyline, then we will need to be prepared to tell it *all!*

The first step in preparing ourselves and the children and families of this generation to be evangelists of the good news will be to *know* it. Then, as we know the story, we need opportunity to *tell* the story. I've come to realize that we need to practice telling the story.

Selling or Storytelling?

When we say the word *practice* in the context of evangelizing, many of us may groan, thinking of the multitude of verses and points that we need to memorize and rehearse. Evangelizing has often gotten a bad rap in churches as well as among the unchurched, simply because it can feel like a sales speech. Just when our listener feels that he or she may have eluded the sell, we begin our upsell strategy, fearing we will lose another one. But what if a new generation, compelled by the metanarrative of Scripture, simply became storytellers? What if the story, so embedded in their hearts and lives, organically manifested itself in winsome prose and verse in everyday situations?

We have been given the gift of teaching a new generation the bigness of God's story while allowing them to find their small place in it. As they do, sharing these two things can become as natural for them as sharing their status on Facebook. It's not a speech they need to memorize, but rather a story they get to live—live out loud in the simplest of terms.

Max Lucado once simplified the bigness of the gospel down to this:

> You come before the judgment seat of God full of rebellion and mistakes. Because of his justice he cannot dismiss your sin, but because of his love he cannot dismiss you. So, in an act which stunned the heavens, he punished himself on the cross for your sins. God's justice and love are equally honored. And you, God's creation, are forgiven.[2]

Wow! That is a gripping rendition of the gospel and only takes twenty seconds to share!

Being a Part of the Big Story

When we embarked on this journey of knowing and telling the gospel, we had to brainstorm practical ways to make the Big God Story come to life for our children and their families. We wanted them to grasp the hugeness of the narrative, yet simplify it for children as young as preschool age. In one of my first attempts to share the Big God Story with our elementary students, I simply printed on pieces of paper the names of individuals, events, and places recorded in poignant moments throughout biblical history. Such people, events, and places included creation, Adam and Eve, Noah, Abraham, Isaac, Jacob, Judah, Joseph, Egypt, Moses, Joshua, the Promised Land, and so on. There was one special piece of paper that was a different color. It was entitled "The Promise."

Then I began to tell the Big God Story. I started with Adam and Eve in the garden and shared how God had a perfect relationship with them and that He loved them. After I shared that Adam and Eve chose to disobey God, I talked about the consequences that He gave them and that they had to leave the garden. But, I said, God made a promise to them that one day a redeemer would come, and that redeemer would conquer sin and give us a perfect relationship with God again. I then picked one child to be the Promise.

I went on to pick children from the audience to come up and hold a particular character's name or be a place where those people traveled to or from—always identifying where the hope of the Promise was at any given time. The kids were captivated as I split the room in two when the twelve tribes of Israel split into the ten tribes in the north (Israel) and the two tribes in the south (Judah). Then I asked where the Promise needed to be at this point. When they all shouted out, "Judah!" I realized that they were finally getting it.

When Jesus was born, I turned the Promise's sign over to reveal the name *Jesus*. The kids had this visual to help them identify that the same promise made in the garden, prophesied and preserved throughout history, was and is Jesus the Messiah. This allowed them to see that the Old Testament and the New Testament are part of one storyline where God always had in mind His remedy to bring us back to a perfect relationship with Him. And then, when Jesus died, they understood "why"—and when He rose from the dead, they cheered!

Next, I invited them to be a part of the Big God Story, helping them see that this story is still being written in each one of us. This story continues until Jesus, the Promise, comes again—and when He does, those who love Him and have accepted His gift of grace for their sin will live with Him in a perfect relationship forever and ever.

From that day on, we continued to seek other creative ways to reinforce the big narrative of God's redemption. We created a physical time line on our wall where kids could see all of history at a glance. We had storytellers tell the story with pictures and other visuals that were attached to a clothesline as the story progressed. One leader told the story using upside-down cups to build a pyramid, showing how each event was tied to all the others. At the end, he gave each child a cup to write his or her name on and then add to the pyramid, showing that we too can be a part of the Big God Story.

Kid-sized Storytellers

Once a child grasps the bigger storyline, it's important to captivate that child into the part that God wants him or her to play in it. One church I know has a "storytelling wall" where kids, after checking in, can simply write how God has been writing their story over the past week or weeks. The leader shared with me some of the storylines written by her elementary students:

> God, I hear You.
>
> You have changed my heart forever.
>
> You are the provider we needed to pay our rent.
>
> God is healer.
>
> God's love changes everything in my life.
>
> I can't stop thinking about You, Jesus.

These kids are becoming living testaments. Think about each of those statements. Who wouldn't want to hear those words from the mouth of a child? Unrehearsed, this leader is giving her children the opportunity to practice being storytellers.

Another church provides opportunities for children to share similar things on a designated storytelling weekend in the main service. During the months that precede the weekend, children can share in a video closet how they see God at work in their lives. There they can record their stories in their own words, and then the stories are edited together for the main service. Their stories serve as a mosaic of encouragement to the rest of the church body.

Children are invited into the greater faith community on days such as these, and they begin to get a glimpse of the grandeur of all that God is about. It won't happen overnight, but I believe this new generation, captivated by the entire Big God Story for the sake of the gospel, has the best chance to reach our lost world and invite everyone in it to play *their* part for *His* glory.

MINISTRY ASSESSMENT

Take time to reflect, respond, and dream about how God might use the Big God Story in your life personally or in your ministry to children and their families.

Reflect

After reading about God's grand narrative of redemption, how has its message had a fresh impact on you? In what areas has God's Spirit convicted you as you have considered how you have lived out your part in His story? Where in your life have you discovered His design for you? Where have you lived out your part by faith? What things might have led you to neglect or discover this part? Spend some time writing an account of your thoughts and reflections.

Respond

Take a few moments to respond to God based on the things He has revealed to you. How do you feel that God would have you respond to the following?

- God is Redeemer.
- God has invited you into His story through grace.
- Jesus is coming again.
- The good news is the entire storyline.

However God's Spirit is speaking to you right now, respond to Him in that with a heart of openness.

Dream

What dreams has God inspired in you for making the Big God Story come to life in your ministry? How can you compel children to find their unique part in it? How might the things He has revealed to you be catalysts to make some adjustments in your ministry to children and their families? In what areas can you make storytelling more of an opportunity for the children in your ministry? Where can your "ahas" be shared or translated into a ministry opportunity?

8

A TIME TO REMEMBER
AND CELEBRATE

An Old Testament Tradition in a
New Testament Context

There comes a pause, for human strength
Will not endure to dance without cessation;
And everyone must reach the point at length
Of absolute prostration.

Lewis Carroll, Phantasmagoria and Other Poems

I recently watched a family as they rushed in late for church, trying feverishly to get all four children checked in to their appropriate
classrooms and scurry off to find a seat in the worship center in order
to participate in what would be just a *portion* of the service. Less than

thirty minutes later, they swooshed down the hallway again to claim their children, chattering about how they were in a hurry because they needed to get lunch, take the oldest brother to soccer practice, and finish those homework assignments that were still hovering over their heads. I was exhausted just watching it. Yet I remember those days when just getting through the day was the goal.

But what about pause? Are families ever allowed to push the pause button and simply "be" and remember their God in worship? What was ironic to me that day was that this family actually *wanted* to do the right thing. They somehow made time to come and worship—to be in the very presence of God in the midst of all they had to do. But sadly, I wondered if they truly had.

Hurried and Hollow

Our children and families live in a hurried world full of noise and busyness. Many are fighting to simply make it through another day. Parents and children alike fall into bed at the end of the day completely spent, longing for rest, to simply awake the next morning and *do it all over again*. And it isn't just our families that feel this hollowness. It is often *our* condition as well! We, who are the ministry leaders, the ones who have been given the sacred charge of leading families—shouldn't we know better? Shouldn't we, of all people, be modeling the life that God has called us to in all of its fullness?

Personally, I have more often than not abandoned the solace of pause for the seduction of the "dream." Now I can justify the dream, because it is a dream for investing in children and families, for helping to build a spiritually healthy generation. Certainly this pleases God, right? I find myself arguing with God at times, telling Him

how much *needs to be done*. Promising that I will rest "as soon as …"
When that day never comes, I find someone whom I respect who
agrees with me, and then off I go, again, running on fumes.

Celebrating the Dream Giver

Is this the life God called us to? Is there something missing in our
modern-day missiology? Have we placed our dreams (no matter how
noble and pure) above the dream God has for us? Bruce Wilkinson, in
his book *The Dream Giver*, said, "If you don't surrender your Dream,
you will be placing it higher on your priority list than God. You will
go forward from this moment with a break in your relationship with
the Dream Giver. Your Dream will become your idol."[1]

　　While God is asking us to cease our work in order to remember
His, He is doing this for our own spiritual vitality. He sets Himself,
instead of the zeal of the dream itself, up as the source of our strength.
He literally seeks to take away our work, to give us something more.
George Müeller, who was "father" to many thousands of orphans in
England during the nineteenth century, once said, "Our heavenly
Father never takes anything from His children unless He means to
give them something better." What's "better" is to fall in line with the
rhythm that God intended for us, *so that the dreams He places in our
hearts will be aligned with His Spirit.*

　　I think it might be time to take a look back at our roots, back
to how God designed the rhythm by which His people would live.

　　In Psalm 145:6–7, David encouraged remembering and celebrating God's character and His works:

　　They tell of the power of your awesome works—

and I will proclaim your great deeds.
They will celebrate your abundant goodness
and joyfully sing of your righteousness.

This pattern is evident in Scripture from the very beginning. In Genesis, the great Creator God paused on the seventh day to remember His work and celebrate that "it was good." Passover was established for Israel so they would remember and celebrate God's great work in delivering His people from the bondage of Egypt. The law regarding the Sabbath acknowledged our need to suspend our human efforts and focus on the holiness of God.

From God's early history with His people, He required celebrations (or festivals) to be part of Israel's natural rhythm of life. And the New Testament record shows that Jesus and the early church kept these celebrations as well. While we are not bound to keep these festivals, knowledge of them enhances our faith. The festivals' symbolism is rich and gives testimony to God's character demonstrated in His work on our behalf.

For a long time, somewhere in the abundance of learning about God's Word, the festivals eluded me. After all, aren't they for the Jewish nation? I've found that most evangelical Christians are unaware of the diverse festivals that create our root system and reveal the very heart of God for us to rest and remember and, of course, to celebrate! Let's take a look at them in their context.

Festivals: Old Testament Context

Several times a year the Israelites gathered together for a festival. In Leviticus 23 the Lord said to Moses, "Speak to the Israelites and say to them: 'These are my appointed festivals ... which you are to proclaim as sacred assemblies'" (v. 2). These seven festivals are the Passover, Unleavened Bread, First Fruits, Harvest (or Weeks or Pentecost), Trumpets, Day of Atonement, and Tabernacles (or Booths).

In addition, the Israelites would gather weekly to celebrate the Sabbath, every seven years for a festival of Sabbath, and every seven sevens (on the fiftieth year) to celebrate the Year of Jubilee. Both the festivals and the times of Sabbath were ordained to help Israel remember what God had done for His people and celebrate His goodness. They were a time for the entire faith community to gather together without the burden of work to simply worship and celebrate. During the festivals, the Israelites ate, danced, sang, played instruments, prayed, and offered sacrifices to God.

Festivals: New Testament Significance

Passover was fulfilled when the Messiah became the sacrificial Lamb, His death as our substitute delivering us from sin and death. The festival of Unleavened Bread was fulfilled because He was a sinless, "unleavened" sacrifice to redeem us from slavery to sin, as the Israelites were redeemed from slavery in Egypt. The festival of First Fruits was fulfilled by the Messiah's resurrection—He was the first to rise from death, and He promises that we who believe will one day rise too. The festival of Harvest began on Pentecost with a harvest of over three thousand souls in one day by the promised Holy Spirit, who continues the great harvest of souls today. Some theologians believe the festival of Trumpets will one day announce Christ's return, while the Day of Atonement will usher in His judgment of the nations. Finally, some also believe that the festival of Tabernacles points toward our eternal home in a new heaven and new earth as we leave behind our temporary dwelling places.

In the chart below you can see that each festival was an opportunity for the faith community to remember and celebrate a specific character quality of God.

Festival	Character of God
Passover	Celebrates God's Deliverance
Unleavened Bread	Celebrates God's Redemption
First Fruits	Celebrates God's Trustworthiness
Harvest	Celebrates God's Provision
Trumpets	Celebrates God's Faithfulness
Atonement	Celebrates God's Righteousness
Tabernacles	Celebrates God's Blessings
Sabbath	Celebrates God's Holiness
Jubilee	Celebrates God's Gift of Freedom

This biblical model of *pausing* reveals how the faith community intentionally stopped and gathered together, both at home and communally, to remember specific things God had done. During these times, the faith community proclaimed how they had seen God's character at work in their lives and offered joyful worship in celebration.

It's a challenging thought to consider how to create this environment for today's children and their families. Outside of a cultural mandate or observance, how do we help this generation take time to be still, to set apart holy space, to simply worship?

I find myself tempted to compete with the pace and provisions the world offers children, to *entertain* them. I want them to enjoy coming to church and to have positive feelings about God, so I sell out what I believe they *need* for what I think they *want*. While avoiding this temptation may be difficult, it is essential for lasting faith formation.

Translating Pause into Ministry to Children and Families

In my current ministry to children and their families, we pause on every sixth and thirteenth week within a quarter to Remember and Celebrate. This weekend is distinct from the others in that we do not cover new material, but rather take time to reflect on how God has been working in our lives in the weeks prior to our meeting together. We tell stories, we sing, we dance, we play games … and of course, we *feast!*

When we first introduced a Remember and Celebrate weekend at our church, the kids were unsure how to share stories or even recognize how God had been at work in their lives. Their stories hovered around such things as praying for sick relatives and hoping that Dad would let them get a puppy. However, as we continued on this path and made this a priority rhythm of our lives together, children began to be awakened to God's Spirit and His work in everyday situations.

Kids Hearing from God

On one Sunday, God's Spirit decided to take us to the next level. A first grader announced during our storytelling time how God had convicted him to give away much of what had been accumulating in his closet and drawers. He confessed before his peers that he had been hoarding, unwilling to share with those less fortunate. After sharing, he confidently took his seat among his peers, and no one moved for what seemed like eternity. Then, the next one got up and shared.

This third grade girl shared that God had been speaking to her, telling her that He wanted her to take better care of her body. He wanted her to be healthy so that she could be all He wanted for her to be in His Big Story. And the stories continued: a young boy was prompted to forgive his unfaithful father; another girl wanted to be bold on her non-Christian campus; and another wanted his dad to know Jesus. In this moment of pause, they were hearing from the Almighty God. His Spirit was moving, and none of us had ever seen anything like it.

Of course it didn't happen overnight. It wasn't even formulaic. We knew this was true because just a few weeks later, in many respects, the sacredness of the former day was lacking in our present response. But we were all eyewitnesses that it *did* happen once, and if it could happen once, it could happen again. We could all testify that God had shown up and moved supernaturally in the lives of our kids.

We've seen this power many times since. As we are faithful to create an environment for kids to stop and listen, to remember and celebrate, God is faithful to show us Himself. Our kids want that. They want the times when, without us telling them, they know that something special has just taken place—and they will never see God or each other again in the same light.

God's Character Revealed

In our ministry we took it a step further. We looked at our annual calendar and considered how we could take the eight Remember and

Celebrate weekends (every sixth and thirteenth week in a quarter) and focus on one of the festivals and the character of God that it displayed. So we plotted out the seven annual festivals (Passover, Unleavened Bread, First Fruits, Harvest, Trumpets, Atonement, and Tabernacles), leaving our final festival as Jubilee! Of course every week is Sabbath, and that gave us plenty of opportunity to identify this one for the kids.

We didn't just *talk* about the Old Testament festival of Harvest. Rather, we shared what the Jewish people did to celebrate God's provision and then used that as a springboard to discuss the ways God is providing for us today. We then gave celebratory thanks. This has become our children's most treasured tradition. Families are even adopting the Remember and Celebrate language and posture in their everyday situations.

What traditions, rituals, and symbols do today's children identify as markers of their faith development? What annual observances create an identity for them? Where in our ministry do all the generations come together to celebrate God's faithfulness? These questions allow us to consider how we might implement this kind of worship in culturally transferable ways.

Transferable Tradition

Recently my husband and I celebrated our wedding anniversary. Usually we go out to dinner and exchange gifts or cards. However, this time we decided to introduce this concept of Remember and Celebrate into our evening. At dinner, I took out a napkin and wrote down the ways God had showed His faithfulness to us in each year of our lives together. After we completed the list of remembrance, the only response was celebration and worship! It was the most meaningful anniversary we have ever experienced simply because we took the time to stop, to pause … and remember.

God ordained this rhythm because active remembrance cultivates relationship. God wants us to look back and recognize His faithfulness, intense love, and personal interaction with His people individually and as a community. When we teach children to pause and remember, we teach them what it means to honor our relationship with God—that intimate relationship in which we speak and He listens, He speaks and we respond.

We desire that a heart of remembering God and celebrating His character will be a part of children's faith formation long after they leave our programs. Translating our traditions and rituals into their daily lives will serve them long after they graduate out of our ministries.

One family I know engages in this type of tradition on an almost nightly basis. As they sit around the dinner table, each person reflects on his or her day. As they recount the ways they saw Jesus in their lives that day, they pause to remember. Then in an act of celebration, they all raise their glasses (of milk, juice, or water) and cheer, "To Jesus!" This fun and impromptu tradition allows young family members to see God's power working in everyday and ordinary life situations.

Faith Develops in Community

God designed us to live within a faith community that remembers and celebrates in order to experience Him in ways that can only happen while we are in close proximity to one another. The faith community creates an environment to equip and disciple parents and children to celebrate God's faithfulness in rich traditions. These traditions offer children a strong sense of identity, security, and belonging.

Every year, children of Jewish heritage participated in the festivals, where they enjoyed the faith community in all of its richness. They ate delicious food, learned and joined in cultural dances, and shared a common experience with people they hadn't seen in perhaps months—cousins, friends, and family members from all over the region. They'd come together to celebrate for somewhere between seven and ten days! Those days together in the faith community were marker points of faith development. It would have been a spiritually shaping experience for kids to live in that communal expression of worship. Today we need to be diligent to ensure that we're creating an environment that offers this kind of community for our children.

Practically Speaking: Leading Kids to Remember

My friend Matt Guevara, a children's pastor in Illinois, took on the challenge of implementing the tradition of remembering and celebrating in community. This was his response:

> The first Remember and Celebrate weekend we had last year was awesome. The highlight of each service was the storytelling time where kids shared their experiences with God. The opportunity to engage in storytelling was brand new to our kids and ministry context; we simply did not have an

environment that fostered this kind of regular sharing and reflection. Last weekend, we decided to use something unexpected to facilitate storytelling: "familywork" (like homework, but for families).

As a team, we created a resource template that would guide kids and their families through a storytelling process that centered on God's work in their lives in preparation for the next Remember and Celebrate weekend. This way they could work on it as a family and come prepared to share when we gathered together as a faith community.[2]

Another children's director in Minnesota, Katie Bliss, has discovered the power in adopting this kind of posture of the heart:

One of the things that Remember and Celebrate weekends have reminded me about is the need to rest, be still, quiet my soul and mind so I can hear the Holy Spirit. I know this is something I need to be doing regularly if not daily, and yet I am a detail list sort of person who often gets bogged down in the tasks of life and forgets.

In our Remember and Celebrate weekends we sit in a large circle as the entire group, and we go around the circle, sharing what God has been doing in our lives. Each child has the opportunity to share but can also pass. Many of the small group leaders have come to me after these weekends and shared with me their pleasant surprise at the evidence that God is working in the lives of kids in their groups. I say surprise because, as you know, sometimes kids can be busy and even look as if they are not paying attention in class, and yet these are the very same kids who have something amazing to share about how God is working in their lives.

I remember one third-grade boy in particular. When it was his turn to share he told us a pretty scary story about the week before and his having to go to the hospital because he had a seizure and couldn't see. He then told the group he prayed and God healed him. There wasn't a doubt in this young man's mind … God heard his prayer, and He answered it. It was awesome to hear such incredible faith come from this child. It was also pretty amazing that we had recently had a lesson that focused on just that point: "God Hears Our Prayers and Answers."[3]

Our children and families are hungry to live out their faith in authentic response to God—and the biblical rhythm of remembering and celebrating offers a vibrant environment for this to happen in community. No wonder they called these times "feasts"!

MINISTRY ASSESSMENT

Take time to reflect, respond, and dream about how God might use this in your life personally or in your ministry to children and their families.

Reflect

After reading about God's design for Sabbath, rest, remembrance, and celebration, how have you been able to create this rhythm in your own life? In what ways do you practically live out these values personally? In your ministry? In what ways has God's Spirit convicted you as you have been awakened to His purposes? Where in your life have you allowed a dream to become an idol in your life personally? In your ministry? Spend some time writing an account of your thoughts and reflections.

Respond

Take some time to respond to God based on the things He has revealed to you. Is this a time of confession or celebration? Is this a time to seek wisdom and guidance? Is this a time for quietness and solitude? However God's Spirit is speaking to you right now, respond to Him in that with petition and thanksgiving.

Dream

What dreams has God inspired in you for remembering and celebrating? Is there a specific story that has come to mind where God has shown His character to you? Is there a particular way that you can mark this victory with celebration either alone or with others? How might the things He has revealed to you be catalysts to begin a new tradition in your ministry to children and their families? Where can your story be shared or translated into a ministry opportunity?

9

WORSHIP AS RESPONSE

Getting to the Heart of the Matter

It is in the process of being worshipped that
God communicates His presence to men.

C. S. Lewis, Reflections on the Psalms

There are seventeen different words in the Bible, in both Hebrew and Greek, that represent the idea of worship. Many of the words that are translated as "worship" in English are related to the nuances of worship, such as glory, honor, reverence, awe, service, beauty, and holiness.

The complexity of the word is perhaps due in part to the majesty of God Himself. How could one word contain the grandeur and depth of our God? Ironically, we find ourselves so often using this word to merely describe the singing portion of our weekend services.

Recovering Worshipper

I have a friend named Matt who calls himself a "recovering worshipper." He confesses,

> Like many, I grew up going to church and thinking that worship was something you did at an appointed time and place and in a particular way. Usually, the place was church and the time was at the beginning of the service before announcements and the message. Then there was the method of worship. Worship was always singing with a live worship band and was usually led by five or six well-dressed singers with amazing voices singing in perfect harmony. The problem for me was not the "how" of worship. The problem came in the "why." The "why" for worship was never incredibly compelling to me. Yes … we worship because God is worthy of our worship … but why before the announcements? Why with three "upbeat praise" songs followed by one "contemplative worship" song? Why was worship always through singing? I always felt like I was worshipping because somebody else decided it was time. There had to be more.[1]

Perhaps you can identify with Matt. You know there is more, and you want that more for the children and families in your ministry.

Because, technically speaking, singing is not worship. Singing is a *means* to worship. Worship is the act of ascribing worth or value to another. Paul spoke of another way to worship when he said that offering our bodies as living sacrifices—all that we do and say—is our spiritual act of service (Rom. 12:1–2). The word for service in the original language is *latreia*, which can also be translated as "worship." Service is a *means* to worship. Kneeling, bowing, and falling prostrate on one's face are also a means to worship.

There are many *means* to worship, but worship occurs only when it is from our heart. To sing may or may not be worshipful; it depends on our heart. To bow may or may not be worshipful; it depends on our heart. And to serve may or not be worship—it too depends on what is in our heart. Is this act or deed motivated by awe, love, fascination, fear, or the grace of God? When it is, then this is deemed true worship by our God.

A Heart's Response

Perhaps this is why Jesus said to His disciples, "If you love me, you will obey me" (John 14:15 WE). He is setting up obedience as an act of (or means to) worship. But it is worship from a heart of *response*. In this case, a heart responding out of love. The woman caught in the very act of adultery was forgiven by Christ and sent on her way. Jesus told her, "Go, and … sin no more" (John 8:11 ESV). Her life of sinning no more would be a worshipful response to God's forgiveness. True worship always comes from a heart that is responding to God.

In Exodus 15, when God led the Israelites across the dry ground of the Red Sea, His people responded by singing songs to Him. In 1 Samuel 7, when God was faithful to deliver His people in battle,

Samuel stopped to respond by setting up the Ebenezer stone. Or look at the people in Acts who witnessed the day of Pentecost. After the Spirit descended upon them, they responded as a community by sharing everything they had for the cause of Christ. Worship is our response to God's power and glory. It's our response to who He is.

Authentic Vulnerability

My friend Jeff mentors young worship leaders. He is tenacious about making sure they know they are neither performers nor simply musicians. To lead worship means to usher people into the presence of God's glory—to allow them to see His holiness, goodness, and love so they can respond to *that*.

Jeff once said that authentic worship brings authentic vulnerability, and authentic vulnerability brings authentic worship. The two are inseparable. We cannot worship God with pride or pretense, and in true worship God gently breaks down our defenses. Jeff added, "We also respond to God in worship because He subjected Himself to the utmost vulnerability by becoming flesh and dying upon a cross."[2]

Children are by nature vulnerable. They are willing (especially in their younger years) to "say it as it is." This must be beautiful worship to God. With pure hearts, they teach us what our heavenly Father is looking for. Then something happens as children get older: they are suddenly concerned with what others think. For all of us, that concern takes up the primary space in our hearts, and our worship is tainted. But what if we cultivated deeper worship opportunities for children that would become solidified in their lives *before* the world did?

Creating Space to Encounter Jesus

In order to seize the hearts of the young, we need to be diligent to create space for them to encounter Jesus. We need to ask repeatedly, "Where are we giving prime real estate in our programming for children to experience and worship God?" We need to provide time, energy, and devotion for children to exercise their prayer muscles and faith muscles in acts of authentic and vulnerable worship. None of us want to program things to the minute with songs, teaching, special effects, games, and crafts without our kids experiencing true worship. Instead, we can take steps to assess our current worship services for kids and ask:

- What would it look like to allow our kids to pause to listen to God?
- In what ways can we give our kids options in how they feel led to respond to God?
- How can we create a place for our kids to write out their prayers and praises?
- Can we provide resources for our kids to journal their thoughts to God?
- Where can we carve out time for our kids to stand up and declare God's goodness and faithfulness, and to celebrate that bold expression?

Tommy Larson, a family pastor in California, said, "We give kids an opportunity to respond because we believe God can and does speak to them. To say it's not possible for kids to hear God's voice is a limitation not on our kids but on God Himself. If He has the power to speak to ravens and tell them to feed Elijah, why couldn't or wouldn't He speak to the creation He loves most?"

Tommy recounted the first time he and his team introduced his elementary kids to the concept of worship as a response:

> I remember the fear I had going into that service. We wanted silence for a few moments after the message to ask the kids to think about God and then to declare one of God's attributes out loud, finishing the phrase, "God is ..." But we had never allowed for that kind of time before, and we had instructed our staff and leaders *not* to lead by example. We wanted the Holy Spirit to be the leader of that time. Stepping back was a huge step of faith for us. We told ourselves that no matter how long the silence was once we set the stage, we would not jump in and fill that silence with our own voices. We knew it would be difficult to resist the urge to jump in, but I don't think we were prepared for the level of difficulty we experienced.
>
> A couple of us stood in the back while the worship leader said, "Let's stop for a moment and think about the amazing characteristics of God. Who is He? What's one word that comes to mind when you think of Him? Who would like to share?" Our kids are talkers, but at that time, asking them to speak in a group was, to them, uncomfortable and scary. We might as well have asked them each to

sing a solo for all of us! So there we were, sitting with fifty kids … in silence. Waiting … waiting. Nothing happened.

Our team sat in the uncomfortable silence, desperately wanting to fix it. But instead we continued to wait and pray. We prayed that the Holy Spirit would lead during this time and prompt kids to stand and declare God's goodness. Then, out of nowhere, a little girl cautiously stood up, hunched over and staring at the ground, and said sheepishly, "God … is … amazing?" As if it were a question. From there another kid stood up and declared, "God is powerful." Then another and another. Suddenly, without any adult leader, kids began to stand and not just say words, but *shout* them—over one another! It wasn't in a competitive way, it was worshipful! In that moment we realized the power the Holy Spirit has to speak, nudge, and guide us all, even at the youngest of ages. We also realized that worship doesn't just happen in a song and that God can be glorified by declaring one simple word.[3]

This illustrates a few very important aspects of worship as response. First there was a conviction that God does and will speak to children. Second, the leadership team was committed to wait on God no matter what happened. They literally put their faith on the line with anticipation that if God didn't show up and prompt a child to speak, then nothing else was going to happen that day. Wow. That's gutsy. And finally, there was a simplicity to the worship. There were no cool band members, no special effects, no bells and whistles—just simple words, and kids ascribing worth to God. Worship.

Preschoolers Too

I remember the week we decided to create space for our preschoolers. It's hard enough for them to just sit for a few minutes and listen to God. But we saw them flexing those little faith muscles, and we wanted them to experience worship, too. So the worship leader asked them to close their eyes and sit quietly. Their eyes were closed so tight (yes, there were some eyes peeking, too), and then the leader said, "You can talk to God, right now and right here. You can tell Him that you love Him or thank Him for loving you, or you don't have to say anything and just listen."

When the service was over, one five-year-old bolted straight out of the classroom when his mom came to pick him up. He said, "Mom, I was praying today in church, and I have to do something for the poor."

She said, "Well, that is amazing. Is that what you learned about today?"

"No, it was about Gideon. But I have to do something for the poor."

So they went home, and this mom cultivated this insight in her little boy. She asked, "What would you want to do for the poor?" As a family they spent much of that weekend discussing it, and he decided that he wanted to raise enough money to buy a water well for a village in Africa. His mom asked him, "How are you going to raise eight thousand dollars for a well?"

He thought and said, "I'm going to do a walk-a-thon." This little boy was adamant that God had called him to raise money and that he was going to do a walk-a-thon. Remember, he's five!

So this mom called our preschool director and asked, "Is there a way that my son can come to all of your weekend preschool services, cast his vision for the first preschool walk-a-thon ever, and invite the rest of his faith community into what God is doing?"

We said, "Absolutely."

So this little boy went to every preschool service and shared, "God told me this in worship response time, and I'm going to do a walk-a-thon, and you can be part of it."

The walk-a-thon was inspiring. Kids showed up to walk, having solicited sponsorships for each lap. Some kids had their trikes, and they went around the track, and some kids made it a quarter of a lap before they got distracted by the flowers or the playground toys. But what was amazing was that this boy continued to walk. He was convinced—the Spirit of God had captured his heart in such a way that he was certain this was what God was calling him to do. And nothing was going to stop him.

So as kids made it one lap or two laps or got hot or went and ate orange slices, he continued to walk until he finished the number of laps he had committed to. Over the next few weeks, everyone brought in money, and we celebrated what God did through this little boy through his time of worship to God. This wasn't led by our staff or encouraged through a church program; this was simply allowing our kids to encounter Jesus.

We gave the kids space and helped them process what it is to hear God's voice, to discern it out of all the other voices that are clamoring for their attention. This little boy heard God's voice, then his mom stepped in and fanned his flame, and then people supported him. There are people in Africa drinking clean water right now because of this little boy. Because of worship.

Impact on Volunteers and Leaders

As time went on, and we were participating in responsive worship in all of our age groups, our volunteers were continually amazed and sometimes wept as they watched the kids respond to the Holy Spirit. Many of our volunteers didn't have this kind of relationship with Jesus in their own lives, and it stirred something in *them*. They began to desire this authentic worship. Often our leaders started responding right alongside our kids.

One leader in particular had her world radically changed by the worship response of a child. Michelle serves in a children's ministry department in Nevada. Michelle and her husband had been having marital challenges that ultimately led to a divorce due to infidelity. Three months after Michelle filed the necessary paperwork, a kindergartner in her children's ministry drew her a picture after leaving the worship service one day. Still in a posture of response, this child felt the urgency to draw a particular picture.

She drew a picture of Michelle, her husband, and their daughter at their home with a big heart around it. This little girl knew nothing of the situation or her family when she gave it to Michelle the next week. When Michelle saw the image, she knew immediately that God was speaking to her. Her bitterness toward her husband began to melt away by God's grace. Eventually, it was this image that led Michelle to write a letter of forgiveness to her ex-husband.

Her ex-husband was stunned to receive the letter and called immediately. In a repentant and humble voice, he expressed his love to Michelle. They both realized that although there was still much to work on, they loved each other deeply. Miraculously, during the week their divorce became final, they started the arrangements to remarry. Today they are remarried and expecting their second child.[4]

These are not just storylines created in Hollywood; these are better. They are true, and they are being written every day in the lives of those who are willing to listen, worship, and respond. I sometimes wonder how much we are missing simply because we neglect this time in our lives.

Worship Beyond Sunday

Our hope as ministry leaders is that the children and families in our ministry would be worshippers long after the final chord is sung on Sunday. We want worship as a response to God to be the posture of their hearts in every situation, every day. As our children begin to understand how God convicts, comforts, and speaks, they begin to understand what being in relationship is all about.

One mom, whose child was given the opportunity to respond to God at church, shared how God was leading her son to respond at home:

> My children were sitting on the living room floor,
> an overturned box of toy cars in front of them.
> They cooperated in deciding on a way to play that

seemed fair to both of them. It was agreed that one of them would take charge of the garage and one would play with the car wash. Then the division of the vehicles began. The plan was that each of them would take turns choosing a car from the pile. Unfortunately, this compromise was easier said than done. My daughter, who is four years older than my son, decided that she should go first. Of course, her first choice happened to be my son's favorite truck. He squealed in protest, but she would not budge.

I heard their voices escalate, and I knew that a fight was brewing. Before I could intervene, my son picked up the nearest car and threw it at my daughter. It hit her head, and she reeled back, stunned, but without tears. Instead, it was my son who began to sob and ran to his room. I followed him, expecting to hear a laundry list of all the things his sister had done to hurt his feelings. Instead, he looked up at me and choked through his tears, "I hurt my sister." The expression on his face made it clear to me just how sad he was. I sat with him while he composed himself and we talked about why it hurt. What my son was feeling was a sign that the Holy Spirit was working in his heart. God was speaking to him, helping him see when his choices were not good. He was there to convict and guide him to a proper response.[5]

Another mom shared with us that something was happening in her child's life in the area of worship. Her three-year-old son was in his car seat while the two of them ran errands. They heard someone on the radio read a Bible passage. At the conclusion of the reading, this mom looked back at her son and saw that his eyes were closed and his hands were held out. She asked her son what he was doing, and he said, "We just heard God's Word, and now it's time to respond."[6]

Since he was only three, I'm sure much of what took place that day was him imitating others, and he was simply responding in ways that he had seen modeled. But I wonder what my spiritual life might look like today if I revered God's Word to the extent that every time I heard it, I considered quiet space in order to see how God wanted me to respond.

Another parent shared how she was having a sad moment because of a conflict with a neighbor. Her daughter saw her teary-eyed and came close. This little girl then said to her mom, "Let's take a moment and listen for God's voice." They did take a moment to listen for God's voice, and this time of stillness lifted her spirits. This mom said she knew that her daughter had learned that expression from the children's ministry and now wanted to create that space at home![7]

Be Still

Where in modern culture do children and their parents have the opportunity to simply be still? Psalm 46:10 says, "Be still, and know that I am God." I love that in the stillness there is knowledge of God. It is not stillness or quietness for the sake of just being still, but for the sake of knowing God. Don't we hunger to know Him? Don't we desperately need to know Him, His voice, His love, His peace?

Think of the families in your church. The crazy, hectic lives they lead drive them away from knowing the depths of God's character. Since worship is a response to who God is, it's more difficult to ever truly worship in our current agendas. So when we consider the family events we might plan, we cannot neglect the fact that families need an opportunity to be still as well.

My friend Dawn is a children's pastor in Kansas. This past year she offered an eight-week Spiritual Parenting class. On seven nights she did the normal training, but on one night, without the parents' knowledge, she decided to do something completely different. Instead of providing the normal DVD clips, teaching, and table discussions, she turned the room into a prayer experience. The room was dimly lit, with different stations to consider God, His faithfulness, their children, and their roles as parents. There were intentional places to read and meditate on Scripture verses pertaining to these things as well. The night was not what they may have *wanted*—they wanted information on how to parent their children—but it was what they *needed*. They needed to be still with God. He spoke. They listened. They spoke. God heard their prayers. God comforted, healed, and encouraged. God was worshipped that night in their responses to Him and in the days that followed in their homes.

Worship Response in the Home

Many families think of "going" to a worship service. It's at a certain place at a certain time. I'm not sure that most parents think they can lead worship in their homes at any time, all the time. Pastor and spiritual formation author John Piper said of the early church's trajectory after the coming of the Holy Spirit, "So you can see what is happening in the New Testament. Worship is being significantly deinstitutionalized, delocalized, de-externalized. The whole thrust is being taken off of ceremony and seasons and places and forms and is being shifted to what is happening in the heart—not just on Sunday but every day and all the time in all of life."[8]

As God poured out His Spirit to His church, He wanted us to experience Him in ways that reached down into the very crevices of our daily living. What better place than in the desolation of our hearts and homes? Our families are hungry for this type of worship and response to a worthy God. They need our support in this because it's foreign, and just as on that first day among the elementary students, it will feel awkward in the beginning. Encouraging families to press on will strengthen their faith and that of their children.

Let's consider a few practical ideas that can help bring worship to the homes of our families.

Conversation Starters

Often parents want spiritual conversations with their children, but they don't know how to enter into them. Parents of preschoolers can do this is by asking "wonder" questions. Here are a few examples:

> I wonder … how do you think God can talk to you?
> I wonder … how did God put all of the stars in the
>   sky?
> I wonder … how does God pay special attention to
>   everyone in the world?

I wonder ... how do you know that God is with
you?

I wonder ... what special thing does God love
about you?

I wonder ... what might Jesus have said when He
was blessing the children?

I wonder ... how does God show you His love?

I wonder ... what do you think God might want
to say to you?

As the child responds, the parent has an opportunity to respond
also. When finished, a parent can simply say, "What can we tell God
right now about how we feel?" As the child answers, that statement
alone can be a response of worship, and the parent can say, "Your
answer is a gift of worship to God." Or the parent and child can
verbalize the worship into a prayer as well.

For older kids, sometimes a "finish the sentence" is a great way
to generate a conversation about spiritual matters without forcing a
"correct" answer. Such statements might include:

If I could be more like Jesus in one way, it would
be ...

The best time I ever had helping someone else was
when I ...

I feel closest to God when ...

When I pray to God, I feel ...

Sometimes I can feel that God wants me to do
something because ...

I know for sure that my prayer was answered when
    I prayed for ...
If I could be known for one thing it would be ...
I think God hears my prayers because ...

Physical Markers

Parents can pray as a response to one of the thoughts that are conveyed in the above conversations. Also, sometimes creating a physical marker is a great way for elementary-aged children to worship. For example, some families have a jar of smooth stones with a permanent marker nearby. When a family member wants to celebrate something about God, they can write on a stone and put the stone back in the jar. When the jar is full, the family can create mosaic stepping stones for the yard and begin another jar of stones to remember God's character in worship.

Prayer Walls

A physical space where prayer is made prominent in the home is a tangible way to allow families to worship together. Some have whiteboards or chalkboards and can write prayers to God for thanksgiving and praise. Others take wooden picture frames (without the glass) and string twine around them in diverse directions, creating a web. Then, with small papers and clothespins nearby, family members can write their prayers and attach them to the twine.

God Is ...

Having a place to simply declare who God is, is one of the most tangible acts of worship. As we ascribe to Him the qualities that only He is, we declare He alone is God. Some families have painted statements of God on a rock outside their house or have a chalkboard dedicated to this. In our home, we had words that describe who God is on our refrigerator. Often as we were making dinner, I would ask my children, "Which one of these words stands out to you today, and why?" Their answers often led us down a path of what they were thinking but also led our time of worship in prayer or thanksgiving at dinner.

Can't Be Contained

There are many other ways families can consider living lives of worshipful response by reading God's Word together, serving together, and choosing something to which they as a family can give sacrificially. However, the difference is that they are not doing these things in order to be "good Christians." Rather, they choose to do these things with a heart of response that cannot be contained.

Remember King David, who broke out dancing in the streets because his gratitude to God couldn't be contained? Children are in the best position to have uninhibited lives of worship, so let's create places in our homes and weekend services where kids can respond to His love and goodness without the barriers that our structures sometimes impose. We have the privilege of allowing them to do what they do best, worshipping Him with their whole hearts!

MINISTRY ASSESSMENT

Take some time to put Psalm 46:10 into practice. Find a quiet place and be still. As you sit in this sacred moment, listen to what God is saying about the worship ministry in your area of ministry.

Reflect

In what ways have you reduced the idea of worship to an event or formula? What are the issues that keep you stuck in these paradigms? What words best describe worship in your area of ministry? Is *response* one of them? What is the condition of your personal life of worship? How is it vibrant? Where is it anemic? What do you sense God saying to you in this moment about these things?

Respond

As you meditate on who God is, what are the words that come to your mind today? Finish this sentence, "God is ..." How has His character shaped you in this past season of life? What is your response to that intervention? To His love? To His grace? Do you feel a humble desire to bow before Him? Do you feel like David, wanting to dance in the streets? How has God awakened you to authentic worship as response so that you can awaken others? What will be your message?

Dream

If the children in your ministry today were released to worship from the inside out at the earliest of ages, how would you envision the church in ten years from now? Twenty years from now? What would the state of our families be if parents and kids didn't simply attend a worship service but lived lives of worship and service? How would our world be different? How can you be a part of this dream?

10

FLYING IN V-FORMATION

Leading in the Midst of Change

*Getting over a painful experience is much
like crossing monkey bars. You have to let go
at some point in order to move forward.*

Unknown

The ink was barely dry on the ministry plan that I was about to submit to my supervisor. It had been months in the making, and I felt satisfied that I had heard from God and knew what He had for us in the next ministry season for our kids and their families. In the midst of transitioning my ministry from a children's focus to a family/parent ministry, I had finally penned by best "next steps."

With excitement I had labored long and hard to put my dreams and visions into tangible process and strategic plans so that others would feel confident in the decisions I had made. Then I received an email to hold off on finishing my ministry plan, because some "changes" were in the works and I would know more as soon as possible.

I sat at my desk in bewilderment. Had I not heard from God after all? Had I wasted my time being diligent when others had procrastinated on the task and now had nothing to lose? Would these changes ultimately mean losing traction on my dreams for my ministry area? I put my plan on pause and waited for those in leadership over me to help me navigate what was to come.

A Changing World

We all live in an ever-changing landscape of children's and family ministry. Just when we begin to think we have a handle on the here and now, someone begins to discuss tomorrow, the new paradigm, or the next ministry season. And the family itself is constantly morphing. Sometimes it feels that by the time we can turn the ship to respond to a felt need, *that need* is obsolete, and two more have taken its place. As Christian leaders, we can find security in the midst of this apparent chaos of change by knowing that God Himself is immutable. A. W. Tozer once wrote that,

> God knows instantly and effortlessly all matter and all matters, all mind and every mind, all spirit and all spirits, all being and every being, all creaturehood and all creatures, every plurality and all pluralities, all law and every law, all relations, all causes,

all thoughts, all mysteries, all enigmas, all feeling, all desires, every unuttered secret, all thrones and dominions, all personalities, all things visible and invisible in heaven and in earth, motion, space, time, life, death, good, evil, heaven, and hell.[1]

Keeping this truth in mind as we explore the subject of leading through change allows us to live in peace, for God is ultimately in control of all the circumstances we call life. In fact, all things that are, were, will be, could have been, and could be, God knows. He is never stunned. He has no need to learn. No need to gather facts.

Psalm 139 reminds us of this incredible thought as well. It tells us that before there is even a thought on our minds, God knows it full well. Accepting this supernatural phenomenon in our lives and ministries, we can embrace the changes that we initiate, as well as those that find their way into our lives without invitation.

V-Formation

I remember sitting at the beach one day, watching a flock of birds flying overhead in a V-formation. In awe, I wondered how they kept it all straight, how they knew where to go and when to change direction. Was one bird leading it all, or did they take turns? I realized this was more of an art than something that had been rehearsed or orchestrated ahead of time. They simply made small, even imperceptible changes along the way. They stayed together, all moving forward, because they were willing to be nimble and pliable. The course was changed on many occasions, but they were able to change with the wind or the circumstances to continue ahead.

Today, during the process of changing children's ministries to make parents a priority, the primary concern is not only to survive but to succeed. And much like those birds at the beach, survival and success are often determined by how we lead and respond to change. It is not something we can rehearse or orchestrate, but understanding how to lead change or how to lead within a season of change is vital to the new generation of children's and family ministries today.

Authentic Transitions

In my experience, it seems that in most cases it's not the change that people find difficult, but the transitions. Change is more physical or situational, but the transition is the psychological *process* we journey through in order to *accept* the state of the new change. In other words, change is an external force, while transition is an internal wrestling. No matter how significant the change may be, unless *authentic transition* takes place in the lives of those involved, that change will not occur.[2]

I've seen authentic transition threatened in a variety of ways. Often, leaders try to plunge ahead too forcibly without establishing a high enough sense of urgency (or need) among the members. In addition, many leaders and pastors underestimate how difficult it is to take people out of their comfort zones and therefore communicate a lack of patience.

I've been guilty of this very thing. I'm an activator by nature, and once I know where I'm going and how I want to get there, I want to do it immediately. I want to change the ministry paradigm, the curriculum, or our programs—and I have good reasons for doing so.

However, I have at times inadvertently created unnecessary anxiety and even squelched the process of successful change altogether by moving too fast or without adequate understanding of the cost of change. I've also used a sense of urgency properly, and it became the very motivation that fueled my team, and our parents, from our present reality to the envisioned future.

Managing Transitions: A Time to Mourn

William Bridges, in his book *Managing Transitions*, outlines a three-stage process in which change and transition take place. The stages are *ending, neutral zone*, and *beginning*. What is intriguing about this model is that it reverses what most leaders expect from those experiencing change.[3]

Consider this situation: you announce that there will be a change in process, policy, or leadership in your children's ministry, and then you give the date in which this change will "begin." You most likely understand that there will be a "neutral zone" in which individuals will struggle in various ways, and much progress will not take place, but then you hope that eventually (and as quickly as possible) there will be an "ending." The process looks like this:

Beginning—Time for People to Process—The End

However, this way of thinking can undermine the success of change in any community.

Think of this same example, but now in *reverse*. Transition starts with an *ending*, the letting go or the death of something. It looks more like this:

The End—Time for People to Process—Beginning

Usually the staff members or volunteers in your community are asked to give up norms, peer groups, work habits, achievements, feelings of competence or respect, or identities. While we as leaders boast of God's vision and better stewardship, members of the group feel the loss of something known and safe. Sometimes when we merely recognize that the grief process is inevitable, others can understand that emotions such as anger, anxiety, sadness, disorientation, and depression are not necessarily a sign of bad morale or insubordination to leadership, but can be a healthy response to an ending.[4]

The *neutral zone* is often referred to as no-man's-land, which is the place between the old reality and the new promise. It is a difficult place for individuals because the old way of doing things is gone, but the new way is not comfortable or available yet. One of the most difficult aspects of the neutral zone is that people don't understand it. They feel disoriented and struggle with self-doubt. Priorities seem overwhelming and under-communicated, and the ambiguities in direction create frustration.[5]

Strong visionary leaders can exacerbate the situation by becoming impatient with the process. I often find myself in this place, because I have been dealing with the thought of inevitable change for many months and sometimes years before unveiling it. By the time those who are the implementers of that change get the signal, I am more than eager for instant results. It's easy to fail to consider the wanderings and disorientation of the neutral zone.

Process Not Just Production

I remember one instance in ministry when I was tasked by the leadership of our church with changing a very popular children's program. The leadership didn't believe it fit our values any longer but were unsure what they wanted instead. After months of assessment and prayer, I knew the direction I wanted to take. Because I did most (if not all) of the emotional and mental processing while seeking God inwardly and in isolation, my decision to make a change came as a shock to the staff and volunteers involved in the program, as well as to the parents and children. It became nothing short of a revolt! To this day, I'm unsure how I ever survived it.

I learned an important lesson during that period of my ministry. No matter how well I am executing the leadership's directives, no matter how much I may feel that I have heard from God and that I am moving in the right direction, I can sabotage this good momentum by not paying attention to the *process* of change. If ever patience is a virtue, it is during a time of transition.

Leading at the Beginning

Beginnings are distinct from "starts" in that starts take place on a schedule as a result of decisions, while beginnings follow the timing of the heart and mind. On the one hand, beginnings mark the end of wandering in the neutral zone, and some greet them eagerly. It's the moment of "Aha, I get where we're going and how I'm a part of getting us there." However, some people fear the beginning because of the demands it will make and the commitment it requires. After all, beginnings represent that the old way is officially over. There is always a gamble in beginnings since there is no way to ensure that the new way of doing things will work.

I have been on both sides of this issue. I have been the one to implement change and feel the excitement for what's ahead, and I have been on the receiving end, licking my wounds, mourning the glory of the days of yore. Sentiment sets in on the latter scenario, and the "remember whens" begin. "Those were the good ole days," we say, certain that it will never be *that* good again. I wonder what God thinks about this. Why would we ever be complacent to the new thing that He is about to do in our midst?

"The End"

The words *the end* mark for us a poetic conclusion to our favorite story or movie. However, have you ever shouted at the screen as the credits popped up because you didn't want the movie to end? You wanted the story line to continue—you wanted to know what happens next. At the end of one such movie I was furious that the director had done this to us. I say "us," but everyone else seemed satisfied with the ending and was leaving the theater. Not me. That was not *the end* as far as I was concerned. It was only the *beginning*.

So there I sat for a few moments, playing out how the plot would go if now in fact this was the new beginning. Upon finding a satisfactory narrative path, I left my seat, having perfectly written out the future for the parties involved. This is not so easy in ministry, but the sentiment remains. Some people see endings as simply that. They pick up their popcorn and move on. Others see endings as tragic and will do anything to prevent the ending from occurring, and still others fight to see the ending as only the beginning of something better.

I have been blindsided by the diversity of responses that can occur during a process of change, even within a single church or ministry team. Often a change occurs because we are new to leading a team and we don't know how each individual will respond, but equally often we are bewildered by someone we know well in our current position and are simply ill prepared for their response.

In one ministry position in which I had been commissioned to lead change, I found every sort of response. I was attempting to bring a culture of spiritual parenting where there had been none. Desiring to see parents called to their rightful roles of spiritually nurturing their children, I began programs, campaigns, and structures that would allow them to become more involved in the spiritual lives of their children.

Some on my team were passive-aggressive, some were aggressive-aggressive, and I even had to deal with a few who were passive-depressive—*just to name a few*. Of course I had those who loved this change and thought that they had just won the lottery, but their joy was soon squelched by the disapproval from the rest of the group. Anticipating diverse responses will help you manage your expectations of the rate and pace of change. (For further resources on how to consider change processes within your ministry, see appendix B at the end of this book.)

Vision, Plan, and Delegation

Bridges suggests four steps in managing the beginning stage of the change process: explain the basic *purpose*, paint a *picture*, lay out a *plan*, and give each person a *part* to play.[6] I think of purpose and picture as one element: *vision*.

The Power of Vision

In *Leading Change*, John Kotter reminded change agents that nothing is more important in the change process than clarifying and communicating the vision. "Vision refers to the picture of the future with some implicit or explicit commentary on why people should strive to create that future," explained Kotter.[7] This is such an essential part of the process because it helps to align and inspire a community into action.

In our ministries, those of us who are responsible for creating vision are ultimately responsible for discerning God's vision. We can never get ahead of ourselves or allow pride to creep into our plans. Seeking God's vision involves understanding that God is always at work around us, and that He invites us to become involved with Him in His work, to come alongside what He is already doing. As Christian leaders, we are tempted to make great plans and merely ask for God's blessing upon them—and then are surprised when the results lack the passion and legitimate change we were seeking. Moses did an excellent job of vision casting when he translated the idea of the Promised Land into the *picture* of a land of milk and honey.

Once people have a picture of the destination, the *plan* to get there becomes of primary concern. This is not a broad-stroke plan, but one with detailed steps and schedules that will allow members to have short-term wins and understand exactly on what things they need to focus.

Give It Away

Lastly, each person needs a *part to play*. Communicating the purpose, picture, and plan are all very inspiring, but until each member has a part to play, true transition will not happen at every level in the ministry.

One of the biggest mistakes I ever made as a leader was to "get it done." By this I mean that "I" got it done. Because leaders can see the future with clarity and focus, and because they tend to be make-it-happen people, when progress doesn't happen at the pace envisioned, it is all too easy to adopt a do-it-myself attitude. "I'll just do it myself" rings in our ears, and it takes enormous discipline to give each team member a part to play. No matter how insignificant the role, everyone must participate.

History, community, camaraderie, and ownership are all by-products of giving leadership and information away. Very little of significance is ever achieved by a lone star or a small subset of a community. Perhaps awe, envy, mistrust, and jealousy are achieved, but nothing noteworthy or praiseworthy comes from hoarded leadership. *Give it away*!

Thus Far the Lord Has Brought Us

It's also important to create short-term wins or quick successes in order to celebrate the progress to date (which is different from declaring victory too soon). Celebration is a healthy and biblical way to remember how far the team has come. How have you marked the miles that you and your team have already traveled? For leaders it is all too tempting to move on to conquer the next mountain without pausing to remember and celebrate all that God has done so far.

Samuel was Israel's priest, prophet, and judge during one of the periods when the Israelites were inclined to "do what was right in their own eyes." After a costly military loss against the Philistines, Samuel said to the people, "If you are returning to the LORD with all your hearts, then rid yourselves of the foreign gods and the Ashtoreths and commit yourselves to the LORD and serve him only, and he will deliver you out of the hand of the Philistines" (1 Sam. 7:3). Israel obeyed, and the Lord gave them victory. Samuel set a large stone in the ground and named it Ebenezer, which means "stone of help," declaring, "Thus far has the LORD helped us" (v. 12). The significance of the moment was not in the stone itself, but in what the stone represented. This monument marked not only God's help in the battle, but His help to the people since they had entered the Promised Land four hundred years before.

Alignment for the Future

Not only does celebration aid the success of leading through change, but unless alignment occurs, change cannot. Alignment is evident when the majority of the community is functioning out of a clear understanding of and commitment to the vision. With this comes a sense of excitement, energy, passion, and even awe, symbolized by the early church in the second chapter of Acts. This first-century church was equipped to meet the demands of reaching the entire world with the message of Christ due to the synergistic manner in which they saw their faith operating.

They were concerned with being of one mind, with making sure that each other's needs were met, and with ensuring they were operating as a "whole" rather than as individuals. The church today often finds herself in competition, judgment, and conflict in the midst of change, without seeing change as an opportunity to become more unified. Although perfect alignment is never achieved, the more quickly and effectively a church ministry can align its plans and vision to the vision of God, the more it will succeed in that venture.

At the Heart of the Matter

The process of change is complex in our children's and family ministries today. It requires great leaders to communicate wise vision and direction to hundreds and even thousands of followers, intent on one purpose. The focused community can ultimately change this generation with God's love and redemptive grace. After all, it was God's plan to seek and save that which was lost by changing individual hearts through the mercy of a forgiving Father. We have the privilege and responsibility of being ambassadors of the transformation process each day to broken families.

When change leaders are consistent in worship, they will experience the holiness of God. In doing so, they become transformed by it and experience His grace. Those who *experience* God's grace are in a position to *give* grace, something that is essential during times of change and uncertainty. When in the midst of planning and change we have hearts of worship, we are more likely to focus on aligning all of our lives, individually and corporately, with the ongoing activity of God among us.

MINISTRY ASSESSMENT

Take time to reflect, respond, and dream about how God might use the process of change or transition in your life personally or in your ministry to children and their families.

Reflect

In light of the role of leadership in the context of change, how have you led well (both in the past and present)? In what ways has God's Spirit convicted you of times or places where you haven't led well? Are there people you need to make amends with? What pitfalls are you most susceptible to? What areas are your strengths? Where do you need God to show up and bring clarity or wisdom today? Spend some time writing an account of your thoughts and reflections.

Respond

Take some time to respond to God based on the things He has revealed to you. What is an action step that you can take this week in each of these areas?

1. Explain the basic purpose for change.
2. Paint a picture of an envisioned future.
3. Lay out a comprehensive and strategic plan.
4. Give each person a part to play.
5. Celebrate the victories to date.
6. Align efforts toward common goals.
7. Engage in a personal life of worship assessment.

Dream

What dream has God given you that will require change for children and their families as you put it into action? How can you begin to implement this dream with others in the community who are walking beside you? How might the things that He has revealed to you be

catalysts to make some adjustments in the way you lead your staff/
volunteers/parents in your ministry to children and their families?
Where can your journey or "ahas" from today be shared or translated
into a ministry opportunity?

11

LEADING A NEW GENERATION

Volunteer and Staff Development

*Coming together is a beginning, keeping together
is progress, and working together is success.*

Edward Everett Hale

Who are the great leaders of our time? Why do you consider them great leaders? Think of a leader who lived and died before you were born, but whose leadership has influenced your life. John Wesley and Martin Luther are two of my heroes. These men lived and died long ago, but their ministry has had significant spillover into mine. Their mentorship of others, their commitment to family ministry before it was chic, and their writings have developed and inspired me. If we

want to leave a legacy as transformational leaders in today's generation, then we must begin with *that* end in mind.

It's easy to get fixated on the *temporal*: the lack of staff or volunteers, the ongoing dilemma of recruiting and training. Some of us
only *wish* we had a staff or volunteers to develop! Yet as important
as recruiting and training are, we must come up from the mire and
have eyes to see something more *eternal*. For me, building teams has
produced genuine fruit that will continue for seasons to come.

Most of us will work with volunteers at one point, and the volunteer generation of today has unique qualities. They are globally
minded, motivated more by significance than position or monetary
gain, and love to be a part of something epic. They see that the church
must serve the gospel, rather than the gospel serving the church. They
can sniff out incongruences like a hound dog. They know when we are
participating in a *good idea* and when we are investing in a *movement*
of God. I want these people on my team! They inspire me.

Solo or Together

I remember a time in ministry when I felt all alone. I had no staff,
and outside of a few faithful Sunday school teachers, I had no true
volunteer base. It became glaring one autumn as I shuttled the last
bit of fall festival paraphernalia to my office at two o'clock in the
morning. Alone. It had been hours since the last family had left with
their children, bags of candy, and grateful smiles of thanks. There, in
the wee hours of the night, with every part of my body in pain and an
abundance of things that still needed to be settled, I slumped down
in my chair in self-pity. Why was I the only one here? Didn't people
care about the children? The ministry? The *Lord*? Okay, perhaps a bit

dramatic, but it was two o'clock in the morning and I was running on about three hours of sleep. It was then that I realized the importance of team. The importance of giving the ministry away—and not just the parts I didn't like doing.

Years later I was in a ministry where God had allowed me to have great support in both staff and volunteers. After an equally work-intensive event, the team had cleaned up everything in record time. At only ten o'clock that night we were done and celebrating the success with a song of praise. We piled our hands together in a circle and shouted out a cheer. Then we jumped into our cars and headed to a twenty-four-hour diner to "remember and celebrate" all that God had done that night. We shared stories and laughed for hours. I still returned home at two o'clock in the morning, but this time I was full of life and joy and a sense of satisfaction that cannot be experienced when one is in the trenches alone.

Old and New Testament Models

Many Old Testament leaders chose their team members to fulfill a *specific* goal. This goal was either commissioned by God or discerned by the leader. The leader articulated it in clarity and detail to those who would share in fulfilling it. Moses chose faithful men to help judge the Israelites in the wilderness. David and his unmatchable mighty men of war conquered some of the vilest armies ever. And Nehemiah and his diverse and talented team rebuilt the temple in Jerusalem against all odds.

Yet Jesus shows us a staff selection process like none other in history. All of history hinged on His choices, and He was intentional about whom He chose to be part of His team. Nowhere in Scripture does Jesus post an ad asking for applications. On the contrary, He was clear about whom He wanted, and He sought each one out with an individual invitation.

Second, although all were invited to follow Him and be changed by God, those twelve men were invited to be part of Jesus's inner circle and His plan to evangelize the entire world. He was tenacious in teaching them, to ensure that they were clear on why He was there and what the mission was.

Not only did He understand their complexities, but He seems to have chosen them on purpose with diversity. He even chose a disciple whom He knew would be the betrayer. Although sympathetic to their faults and weaknesses, Jesus never allowed his disciples to use those as excuses to be stagnant in becoming more like the Father. His faithful example was indelible on their hearts and minds, and when He returned to heaven, He sent His Holy Spirit to abide with and in them to ensure the mission would continue.

In both the Old and New Testament examples, we see three aspects for developing a team or staff:

- INSPIRING a team toward the goal
- EQUIPPING the team precisely for that goal
- SUPPORTING the team and situation for the long haul

So how can leaders today, who long to effectively nurture their staff and volunteers for spiritual formation, also develop them to accomplish ministry goals? Let's unpack these questions in light of the three aspects of staff development gleaned from Scripture.

Inspire, Equip, Support

I like to think of ministry in terms of "buckets." It helps me compartmentalize the aspects of leadership. To inspire means that we will not barge into our mentor and leadership relationships with a huge to-do list, but rather that we will take the time to inspire people toward an envisioned future, allowing them to be captured by the passion of the mission.

In addition we will seek to equip those in our care. We need to consider what kind of training will allow them to be productive and successful in their positions. If they don't succeed, we must assume part of the responsibility if we have not equipped them with all the necessary resources we have at our disposal.

And support can often be weak in our ministries. Where does one go in grief, sin, crisis, mourning, or simply a bad day? Where does one go to rejoice, celebrate, get motivated, or share an audacious idea? It should be to the leader, shouldn't it? As we investigate the best practices in ministry leadership, let's consider the words *inspire*, *equip*, and *support* as our backdrop.

Inspire

People are inspired by vision. A vision paints a captivating picture of an envisioned future and clearly articulates the part that each one can play in attaining the desired goal. Many management books, both in the secular and Christian fields, make no distinction between vision and mission. However, I believe there is a distinct difference between them, and defining them will aid staff development and goal setting.

When we talk about vision we are referring to the foresight of something that could be. The visionary sees down a path—sometime in the future, past hindrances, obstacles, and problematic issues—to a possibility. Leaders envision, for the rest of us, what this place looks like, and they begin to cast that vision to those who are willing to work toward making that vision a reality. The language used to describe this place is called a vision statement. This statement should be simple and yet inspiring, since this is the wellspring from which all other issues in goal setting flow.

An example of this might be: *"We exist to see a generation of parents spiritually nurture their children into authentic and lasting faith."*

A mission differs from vision in that it gives *purpose* to an organization's vision. It usually tells us *how* we will arrive at the articulated vision and *why* we would consider toiling to do so. It is descriptive in language and should also inspire the hearer.

An example of this might be: *"We will make mentoring parents our primary ministry by inspiring, equipping, and supporting them above all other endeavors."*

As a leader, I have discovered that without an inspiring vision and a tangible mission plan, people will not follow me. We may have the position or title of "leader," but we will not successfully lead without these two components. I can remember on many occasions praying for God to give me clarity and creativity to inspire my team. What words, settings, tangible exercises, or objects would best help me communicate my vision?

There was one season of ministry when I needed to lead an existing ministry team from focusing on children's ministry exclusively to focusing more on family ministry. I chose to take the entire team away overnight so that we would have an extended time, without interruption, to discuss the new vision, as well as to determine our mission to get there. I chose the metaphor of a "bridge" in order to inspire my team. At the beginning of each of our sessions, I told a story of a real bridge, how it was built, the challenges the builders faced, what sacrifices they made, and what the benefits were once it was completed.

A bridge connects two things that were not previously connected and makes it possible to get there. The vision in this case was the piece of land that we were not yet connected to, and what could happen once we were connected became our envisioned future. The bridge itself was our mission. How would we get there, how long would it take, what obstacles or sacrifices would have to be accounted for in order to succeed? This metaphor gave us common language and a visual understanding of our goal. We were united and inspired after our time together to build a bridge from children's ministry to family ministry together as a team.

Equip

Once the leader of an organization clearly communicates the vision for the future and the mission has been determined, the task of equipping the team should be next. To equip those under our care is vital to the success of the mission. Often we are energized by the leader's inspiration but soon find ourselves disappointed that we simply can't get there from here. Equipping a team takes much more effort than the prior step of inspiration and can even be frustrating for the visionary leader who just wants everyone to get going and "do their job" without hand-holding. On the other hand, the "trainer" type of leader thrives on equipping but may have forgotten to properly inspire. Both are needed to lead a team effectively.

Setting core values as the first step of equipping allows each person to know what guardrails will govern the process ahead. These values often determine budgets, staffing, and conflict management among other issues and should be agreed upon by the key stakeholders in the ministry. Finding creative ways to enforce and breed deeper understanding of these goals keeps the values from simply becoming another list that gets tossed away in some drawer. In my ministry, I have used case studies, brainstorming exercises, and TV-style games to make knowing and understanding the goals fun and rewarding. Although we are having fun, team members always share that they learn something new or afresh by our exercises.

Another component of equipping is goal setting, but goals should not be formulated until vision, mission, and values are determined. It is tempting, however, to rush to goal setting because we have a natural tendency to want to get to the tasks of daily ministry. This can be dangerously shortsighted without the proper formulation of the broader issues that the big picture provides.

Goals should be strategic, measurable, and attainable. Unlike a to-do list (which is a common pitfall that I find myself fighting against), goals should be challenging enough to take the whole of the specified period of time—usually one year—and yet realistic enough to attain in that time frame.

For instance, "*Start a memory verse program*" is something you could put on a task list, but it would not serve as an effective goal. A goal might be worded like this: "*Review the age groupings in the children's departments over the next six months, in order to develop an age-appropriate program for Scripture memorization that follows week-end curriculum for ages six to ten.* " The latter language gives *strategy* because it is linked to current curriculum, *measurability* because it gives a six-month review time followed by an implementation program, and *attainability* because the group is a reasonable size (ages six to ten).

When equipping my team, I constantly ask myself how I can assist each person's development. Taking an assessment of spiritual, mental, professional, or personal development has led me to use my budget (or find donors) for educational classes, personal coaching, books, or meetings with high-capacity leaders, to strengthen my team members in their roles. Effective equipping takes prayerful consideration and careful information gathering in a posture of love and respect.

Support

To support my team members means that I am with them in this endeavor for the long haul and that we are monitoring ourselves as individuals and as a team. Kenneth Gangel suggested that "goal achievement moves forward step by step, and its progress must be monitored."[1] He provided the framework of *evaluation, reinforcement,* and *reward.* Evaluation must be done regularly by the entire team. A weekly time for reinforcement, when we remember the goals and have accountability for their progress, builds trust among team members. Reinforcement can come in the form of monthly one-on-one times or staff meetings, where each member reviews the current progress toward completion. This time of reinforcement can also serve as inspiration and a time to realign efforts.

Reward is a time for members to celebrate, either verbally or tangibly, through an event that acknowledges the significant steps made toward the goal.[2] One of my favorite things to do with my team is celebrate. We will "afterglow" after an event, recounting God's faithfulness and affirming the parts that each person played. We have on occasion even taken a workday to play—to refuel and have fun together. Creating traditions is a great way to support those in our care, as we strengthen the essence of being a "tribe" with practices that make us feel we belong. For example, we sing the Doxology after each of our staff meetings and our big events. In doing so, we remember that it is God who deserves all the praise and glory.

Choosing the Team

Of course, we cannot inspire, equip, or support until we choose our team. We can never forget how Jim Collins, in his best-selling book *Good to Great,* put it: "First Who … Then What." Collins researched a set of elite companies who made the leap from good to great results and then sustained those results for over fifteen years. He found that it mattered *who* was "on the bus."[3] Sometimes we get caught up in the numbers, but perhaps you have the one team member who is more valuable than any mediocre dozens.

One of the most critical choices a leader can make in the church or organization is whom he or she chooses to be part of the staff (or volunteer staff). Often, we are tempted to take the first person or résumé with a beating heart and a willingness to work for the salary that is being offered. Naively, we think things will be easier this way, and we have simplified things by moving quickly in order to get back to the "more important" issues. The wise leader is convinced that staffing is the "more important" issue on which all other issues hinge.

Hiring Disaster

I once hired a staff member who looked perfect on his résumé. What leader wouldn't want this capable, talented, and educated person? I neglected to do adequate homework, consult his former employers, or ask my team for their opinion. It was an immediate disaster. Upon his arrival to our team, I knew this was not a good fit. He lacked the tenacious passion of our current "tribe" and insulted our practices with his oozing pride. He was rude, condescending, and abrasive. What had I done?

I tried desperately to make a bad situation better, but inside I knew he was wrong for our team. What was worse was that I had hired him from out of state, and "returning him" would not only devastate his family but also expose the glaring weakness that I had not hired well. In this situation, God's grace actually moved me before moving him, but the sting of that poor leadership decision has motivated me to not be wooed so easily with the outside wrappings in potential hires.

With the wrong people on the "bus," as Collins described, leaders deal almost exclusively with issues of supervision, management, motivation, correction of errors, and lack of competence. These erode the organization's productivity and hinder the leader from doing what only he or she can do. Collins warned that the main point of staff selection is not just assembling the right team, but getting the right people on the bus (and the wrong people off) *before* you figure out where to drive it.[4]

It's crucial both to hire the right people and to identify the wrong people who currently have a seat on the bus. For churches, this can be a serious ethical and spiritual dilemma. The church is supposed to be a *safe* place that is full of love and grace. It is a *family*. However, the church today is also a vibrant organization with accountability to goals and objectives, budgets and boards. How can we reconcile the ideal of family (which you can never be kicked out of) with the reality of an organization (from which you can be removed at any time)?

Delegate or Dynasty?

The right people have ownership of where they are going. In fact, they are a large part of figuring out the right path to get there. A leader of great people will set forth a basic goal or elevating idea and allow the staff to pool resources, gifts, and creativity on what exactly that looks like and how to get there. This model takes an effective but humble leader who is willing to allow his or her staff to share in the molding of the vision.

This model, as opposed to that of a more typical executive leader, has lasting greatness because the goal is in the *very DNA* of every individual working on the project or goal. The more typical executive leader will appear successful and may even create a dynastic feel during his leadership, but the many worker-bees he has enlisted to achieve "his" goal will be left visionless when this leader leaves or retires.

Great leaders, said Seth Godin in his book *Tribes*, give leadership away. They are not concerned with who gets the credit or that they themselves are not being given greater opportunities by those above them. They are more concerned with the mission of the tribe. They want the mission to succeed and those around them to succeed as well. Godin shares that our world is in desperate need of people who will lead, and we cannot afford to cower in fear that we may make mistakes. We will make mistakes. So what? Let's get on with the mission at hand, learning and leading from those very mistakes with greater clarity and confidence.

In our ministry to children and their families, we cannot afford for our influence to benefit others only for the short duration of our work. We must be willing to choose the individuals with enduring character qualities and gifts to contribute wholeheartedly to the church's mission if we are going to change this generation for the sake of Christ. We must have eyes to see beyond the here and now, and beyond who gets the "credit," in order to build lasting teams that, with or without our leadership, understand the mission and will be dedicated to its success.

The Art of Replication

Volunteer deficit is a huge issue in our ministries. I can think of all the tactics I used to attract volunteers over the many years of ministry to children because of this overwhelming need. Looking back, no matter how creative my methods were, they simply were never enough. I remember the feelings of discouragement every weekend, when a volunteer was a no-show or we had to close a classroom due to the lack of volunteers. I desperately wanted to work with dedicated people who were serving out of a calling instead of guilt from a pleading weekend announcement.

About five years ago, I was serving as the Family Ministry Director, leading a team of about ten. One week, after our "recruitment

Sunday all-church announcement," I saw my staff members' disappointment with the amount of response cards. I could tell that they were beginning to lose hope and, worse, lose faith in our mission to children and their families. I had an idea! What if we changed our approach? What if instead of merely trying to recruit and train more volunteers by ourselves, we chose to intentionally invest our time in the replication of others like us?

At the core, this is the idea of mentorship or discipleship. In the model of recruiting, the person on staff is central (like the axis on a wheel), and all energy or success comes from the abilities of that person. In replication, the person on staff serves as a catalyst to awaken another like-minded individual, who will in turn reproduce himself or herself in another after a period of time. While the mathematics of recruiting is addition, the mathematics of replication is multiplication.

With this idea ignited in my mind, I offered an invitation to my staff to attend a dinner celebration at my home. Each staff member was invited to a dinner taking place one year from the day the invitation was made. The ticket to the celebration was "a person"—someone in whom my staff had replicated themselves. Once the invitation was made, not much was ever discussed about that dinner—but it was there on our calendars, staring at us. With a challenge ahead of my staff and a year to complete it, my team set out to accomplish the task, each with different approaches.

A year later, my team of ten had almost doubled in size (not everyone accomplished the goal, which meant not every staff member was allowed to attend the dinner—much to their dismay). We spent time eating, celebrating, and storytelling, and then ended the night with my staff members affirming their volunteers for the ways they had seen dedication and growth in them over the past twelve months.

It was a powerful night. We looked around and realized that we were not alone. Not only had each person replicated himself or herself in another, some of those who had been invested in had already begun the process as well ... and those others were with us too. We called these people our "grandkids." Next, we gave the commission for each of us to go find another and repeat the process. Little did we know that within just eighteen months, our senior leadership would decide to expand to a multicampus model, staffed with volunteers rather than paid staff. While many departments found themselves desperate for leadership, God had gone before us to provide a "deep bench" of passionate individuals to lead each of our campuses.

We realized that recruitment will always be necessary, but instead of merely filling a spot simply for the sake of getting by, we now have a small army of people who stand alongside us in awakening others.

Communicating the Goal

Once the team has been chosen and inspired, equipped, and supported, ongoing clarity in mission is essential to success. Think about your team as it is today. Can they articulate the goal? Is everyone doing a lot of "good stuff," or are they aligning their efforts toward a vision? A mission? It is tempting to believe that tireless effort equals achieving a goal, but it doesn't. Think of the *missions* that were set forth in Scripture for a people called to the *vision* of salvation:

- The mission of leaving one's home to be a group
  of people set apart (Abraham)

- The mission of living as holy people in the wilderness, trusting in God alone as their source of provision (Moses with the children of Israel)
- The mission of completely purging Canaan of unholy nations in pursuit of the Promised Land (Joshua and the twelve tribes)
- The mission of rebuilding the city of Jerusalem and its walls (Ezra and Nehemiah)
- The mission of following Jesus and His new covenant (the twelve disciples)
- The mission of proclaiming the gospel in the power of the Holy Spirit until Jesus returns (the Great Commission)

Each of these missions had clear, defining guidelines. Abraham was to leave his land, trust completely in the birth of a son in old age, and wait twenty-five years for the fulfillment. Moses was given the Ten Commandments, among other Jewish laws, to govern the Israelites' time together as a holy community. Joshua was given strict instructions for conquering the land and would prosper only according to the standards given. Ezra and Nehemiah faced opposition but held firm to the focus of a holy city in order to have a place of worship for their people. The disciples were instructed countless times on what it meant to be a disciple. And those filled with the Spirit of God continue to be instructed throughout the New Testament on what it means to walk in step with Him for the sake of the gospel.

Clarity of mission brings unity, as well as weeds out those who are just along for the ride. It allows a leader to look each person in the eye and say, "Are you in?" Those who are not will eventually self-select out, and those who are will continue to add even more clarity to the mission as they pursue it themselves.

Staying the Course

Moses, Joshua, Isaiah, Jeremiah, Nehemiah, Jesus, Peter, and Paul committed themselves to the long haul of ministry with those entrusted to their care. Each of them had ample opportunities to get fed up and walk away. However, each of these men recognized God's specific call on their lives, and only God could release them from their leadership positions.

As Christian leaders mobilizing diverse staffs in the twenty-first century, we have been commissioned to lead as long as God calls us to that particular ministry. The people who have had the deepest impact on our lives and ministries are not necessarily those who have wowed us with their talent or insights, but rather those with whom we have simply done life. They have been there, encouraging and comforting through the difficult times and cheering us on from the sidelines during our fifteen minutes of fame. They see us for who we are, and they accept both the most radiating qualities of our Father in us and the qualities that are far less than we hoped anyone would ever discover. These people love us anyway.

At the end of the day, year, or ministry season, staff members are affected most by the presence of abundant love. There are many staff development models in the world of management, but the model that most reflects Christ, the model that most winsomely draws others to become like Him, is the model of love. We can't afford not to love, and we can't afford for our staff members not to be transformed by it!

In chapter 5 I shared with you the vision we had in our ministry at that time. We imagined a generation of children and students worshipping from the inside out, possessing a kingdom mind-set, living with global awareness, knowing God and His Word, obeying Him in the power of the Spirit. What is *your* vision? What is the *more* you're dreaming of for the generation entrusted to you? Let me encourage you to hoist up your sail—it's time for God's Spirit to blow!

MINISTRY ASSESSMENT

Take some time to consider your leadership style and the culture of leadership in your church or ministry.

Reflect

Think back upon your seasons (or season) of ministry. How have you led? In a team? In isolation? What are the emotions that surround each of those words? What factors contributed to your leading in this way? What changes do you desire to make? In what areas can you grow? In what areas can you celebrate? How has your role served to inspire those in your care? Equip them? Support them?

Respond

What action steps do you feel led to make? When is a good time to implement these changes? Who are the key people with whom you will share your findings today? Do you need a time of solitude and prayer to confess, process, or celebrate with your heavenly Father? Is there something tangible that could mark this season in your ministry to remember your journey in this respect?

Dream

What dreams does this evoke in you? As you complete this book and the assessment of your ministry, you have probably accumulated many dreams. Which ones are Spirit-led and worthy of your pursuit? How will you begin your journey? What words will describe you and your ministry when you have arrived at your ultimate envisioned future? What word best describes your awareness that even when you have arrived at the pinnacle of your dream, God still has more dreams for you?

APPENDIX A

THE TEN ENVIRONMENTS

1. **Storytelling**. The Big God Story gives us an accurate and awe-inspiring perspective into how God has been moving throughout history. It is the story of redemption, salvation, and hope and tells how we have been grafted into it by grace. It further compels us to see how God is using every person's life and is creating a unique story that deserves to be told for His glory.

   "God has a big story, and I can be a part of it!"

2. **Identity**. This environment highlights who we are in Christ. According to Ephesians 1, we have been chosen, adopted, redeemed, sealed, and given an inheritance in Christ—all of which we did nothing to earn. This conviction allows children to stand firm against the destructive counter-identities the world will offer.

   "I belong to God, and He loves me!"

3. **Faith Community**. God designed us to live in community and to experience Him in ways that can happen only in proximity to one another. The faith community creates an environment to equip and disciple parents, to celebrate God's faithfulness, and to bring a richness of worship through tradition and rituals that offer children an identity. Our love for each other reflects the love we have received from God.

"God's family cares for each other and worships God together."

4. **Service**. This posture of the heart asks the question "What needs to be done?" It allows the Holy Spirit to cultivate in us a sensitivity to others and focuses on a cause bigger than one individual life. It helps fulfill the mandate that as Christ-followers we are to view our lives as living sacrifices that we generously give away.

"What needs to be done?"

5. **Out of the Comfort Zone**. As children and students are challenged to step out of their comfort zone from an early age, they experience a dependence on the Holy Spirit to equip and strengthen them beyond their natural abilities and desires. We believe this environment will cultivate a generation

that, instead of seeking comfort, seeks a radical life of faith in Christ.

"God transforms me when I step out in faith."

6. **Responsibility**. This environment captures the ability to take ownership for one's life, gifts, and resources before God. A child must be challenged to take responsibility for his or her brothers and sisters in Christ, as well as for those who are spiritually lost. We hope the Holy Spirit will use this environment to allow each child to understand that God has entrusted His world to us.

"God has entrusted me with the things and people He created around me."

7. **Course Correction**. This environment flows out of Hebrews 12:11–13 and is the direct opposite of punishment. Instead, biblical discipline for a child encompasses a season of pain, building up in love, and a vision of a corrected path for the individual with the purpose of healing at its core.

"When I get off track, God offers me a path of healing."

8. **Love and Respect**. Without love, our faith is futile. Children need an environment of love and

respect in order to be free to both receive and give God's grace. This environment declares that children are respected because they embody the image of God. We must speak *to* them, not *at* them, and we must commit to an environment where love and acceptance are never withheld due to one's behavior.

"God fills me with His love so I can give it away."

9. **Knowing**. Nothing could be more important than knowing and being known by God. We live in a world that denies absolute truth, yet God's Word offers just that. As we create an environment that upholds and displays God's truth, we give children a foundation based on knowing God, His Word, and a relationship with Him through Christ. God is holy, mighty, and awesome, yet He has chosen to make Himself known to us!

"God knows me, and I can know Him."

10. **Modeling**. Biblical content needs a practical, living expression in order for it to be spiritually influential. This environment gives hands-on examples of what it means for children to put their faith into action. Modeling puts flesh on

faith and reminds us that others are watching to see if we live what we believe.

"I see Christ in others, and they can see Him in me."

IMPLEMENTING A SPIRITUAL FORMATION APPROACH TO FAMILY MINISTRY

As you begin to implement a spiritual formation approach to family ministry in your church, the following questions may be useful in these various discussions:

Church Staff and Volunteers

- In what ways will we need to structure our weekends to accommodate creating space for our children/students to experience God and His Word?
- How will we communicate these goals to our parents and children/students?
- How will this affect the overall annual calendar?
- Are there any events, practices, curriculum, or structures that *violate* these principles? If so, what are they? How will we go about revising or eliminating them?

- Are there any events, practices, curriculum, or structures that are *missing* that would support these principles?
- What are we *willing* to give up or sacrifice in order to make this a reality?
- What are we *unwilling* to give up or sacrifice?
- In what ways have we been unintentionally blinded by tradition, existing practices, or curriculum that we need to abandon immediately?
- How can we ensure that we are not merely adding on spiritual formation and family ministry, but that we are fundamentally adopting a new approach to thinking and being?

Parents

- How will parents need to be inspired by this philosophical direction? Who is responsible for this inspiration, and how will it be unveiled and executed?
- How will parents need to be equipped? What kinds of events, information, and opportunities will be available to ensure that every parent understands the philosophy and has the opportunity to be empowered to implement it in their home?
- What resources will be needed to equip and support our parents? Financial? Time? Staff? Outside speakers/resources? Curriculum? Website?

- What specifically will be expected from our parents?
- How will we communicate with our parents on a regular basis and give them updates?
- How will parents offer feedback to us?

Children/Students

- How will we inspire and communicate a new path of spiritual formation to our children/students?
- In what ways will we adapt our language in order to make sure that all grades participate and understand the path before them?
- What are the desired outcomes of our children/ student communities in this paradigm?
- In what way will we solicit feedback from them, if any?
- How will we discern the diverse but complimentary roles of church and home in this model? Who will be responsible for articulating each role in the life of a child/student?

NOTES

Chapter 3: An Awakening to Parents as Primary

1. George Barna, *Transforming Children into Spiritual Champions* (Ventura, CA: Gospel Light, 2003), 28.
2. Patti Fenton, conversation with the author. Used with permission.
3. Mark DeVries, *Family-Based Youth Ministry* (Downers Grove, IL: InterVarsity, 1994, 2004), 102.

Chapter 4: Faith in Formation

1. Kit Rae (lecture, David C Cook Family Ministry Conversation, Costa Mesa, CA, November 2011). Used with permission.
2. A. W. Tozer, *I Call It Heresy!* (Rockville, MD: Wildside, 2010), 11.
3. Dallas Willard, *The Great Omission* (New York: HarperCollins, 2006), 69.
4. John Coe (lecture, Talbot Theological Seminary, 2007). Used with permission.

Chapter 5: When Jesus Gave Us Something "Better"

1. Francis Chan, *Forgotten God* (Colorado Springs: David C Cook, 2009), 15–18, 32.
2. John Coe (lecture, Talbot Theological Seminary, 2007). Used with permission.

Chapter 7: Finding Your Place in the Big God Story

1. Used with permission.

2. Max Lucado, *Great House of God* (Nashville, TN: Nelson, 1997), 16.

Chapter 8: A Time to Remember and Celebrate

1. Bruce Wilkinson, *The Dream Giver* (Colorado Springs: Multnomah, 2003), 126.

2. Matt Guevara, forum discussion on the David C Cook Tru website. Used with permission.

3. Katie Bliss, forum discussion on the David C Cook Tru website. Used with permission.

Chapter 9: Worship as Response

1. Matt Barnes, conversation with the author. Used with permission.

2. Jeff Fernandez, conversation with the author. Used with permission.

3. Tommy Larson, email to the author. Used with permission.

4. Used with permission.

5. Used with permission.

6. Used with permission.

7. Used with permission.

8. John Piper, *Brothers, We Are Not Professionals* (Nashville, TN: B&H, 2002), 232.

Chapter 10: Flying in V-Formation

1. A. W. Tozer, *The Knowledge of the Holy* (New York: HarperCollins, 1961), 56.

2. William Bridges, *Managing Transitions* (Philadelphia: Da Capo, 1991, 2009), 3.

3. Bridges, Managing Transitions, 5.

4. Bridges, Managing Transitions, 7.

5. Bridges, Managing Transitions, 8.

6. Bridges, Managing Transitions, 60.

7. John Kotter, *Leading Change* (Cambridge, MA: Harvard Business Review, 1996), 68.

Chapter 11: Leading a New Generation

1. Kenneth Gangel, *Team Leadership in Christian Ministry* (Chicago: Moody, 1997), 281.

2. This concept comes from a class in which the author participated.

3. Jim Collins, *Good to Great* (New York: HarperCollins, 2001), 41.

4. Collins, *Good to Great*, 41.